Zorra Township Ontario in Colour Photos, Saving Our History One Photo at a Time

Photography
by Barbara Raué
©2019

Series Name: Cruising Ontario

Book 240: Zorra Township

Cover photo: 70 Ross Street, Embro, Page 24

©All the photos in this book have been taken with my cameras. I own the rights to them.

Series Name: Cruising Ontario, Saving Our History One Photo at a Time in colour photos

Books Available in Alphabetical Order:
Aberfoyle, Acton, Ajax, Alton, Amherstburg, Ancaster, Arthur, Auburn, Aylmer, Ayr, Beaver Valley, Belfountain, Belgrave, Belleville, Bloomingdale, Blyth, Brantford, Brockville, Burford, Burlington, Caledon, Caledonia, Cambridge, Carlow, Cayuga, Chatsworth, Cheltenham, Clifford, Colborne, Collingwood, Conestogo, Delhi, Dorchester to Aylmer, Drayton, Drumbo, Dundas, Dunlop, Dunnville, Eden Mills, Elmira, Elora, Embro, Erin, Essex, Fergus, Fort Erie, Georgetown, Goderich, Grimsby, Guelph, Hagersville, Haldimand County, Hamilton, Hanover, Harriston, Hespeler, Ingersoll, Inglewood, Innerkip, Jarvis, Kingston, Kingsville, Kitchener, Lake Superior, Lincoln, Linwood, Listowel, London, Lucknow, Merrickville, Mono, Mount Brydges, Mount Forest, Mount Pleasant, Neustadt, New Hamburg, Newboro, Newport, Niagara-on-the-Lake, Niagara Falls, North Bay, Oakville, Onondaga, Orangeville, Orillia, Oshawa, Otterville, Owen Sound, Palmerston, Paris, Parry Sound, Pelham, Perth, Peterborough, Petrolia, Pickering, Port Colborne, Port Elgin, Port Hope, Port Perry, Portland, Preston, Rockwood, Sarnia, Sault Ste. Marie, Seaforth, Sheffield, Shelburne, Simcoe, Smiths Falls, Smithville, Southampton, St. Catharines, St. George, St. Jacobs, St. Marys, St. Thomas, Stoney Creek, Stouffville, Stratford, Strathroy, Sudbury, Tavistock, Terra Cotta, Thamesford, Thunder Bay, Tillsonburg, Toronto, Uxbridge, Waterdown, Waterford, Waterloo, Welland, Wellesley, West Flamborough, Westport, Whitby, Windsor, Wingham, Woodstock, York

Book 238-239: Ingersoll
Book 240: Zorra Township

Table of Contents

Embro	Page 5
Medina	Page 31
Lakeside	Page 32
Uniondale	Page 33
Harrington	Page 36
Kintore	Page 38
Thamesford	Page 40

Zorra is a township in Oxford County in south-western Ontario. A predominantly rural municipality, Zorra was formed in 1975 through the amalgamation of East Nissouri, West Zorra and North Oxford townships. It is best known for the Highland Games weekend held each summer in Embro, celebrating the heritage of the Scottish pioneer families. The township comprises the communities of Banner, Bennington, Brooksdale, Brown's Corners, Cody's Corners, Dicksons Corners, Dunn's Corner, Embro, Golspie, Granthurst, Harrington, Harrington West, Holiday, Kintore, Lakeside, Maplewood, McConkey, Medina, Rayside, Thamesford, Uniondale, Youngsville, and Zorra Station.

Among the earliest settlers of Zorra Township, were United Empire Loyalists from the New England States. Zorra was first surveyed in 1820 and Embro became a separate municipality in 1858. Embro is located on a branch of the Thames River. The first buildings were two distilleries owned by McDonald and Crittenden.

Flour, grist and oatmeal mills were built. John McDonald built a carding and cloth factory. Businesses started up: watchmaker and jeweler, boots and shoes, eight blacksmith shops, wagon and carriage makers, tinsmith, carpenters, potash manufacturer, four general stores, two cabinet makers, undertaker, three doctors, and a pump manufacturer. In 1875, Embro had two newspapers, "The Planet" and "The Review", with a third added in 1880, "The Embro Courier". The Embro Public Library started as a Mechanics Institute in 1882; it became a public library in 1895.

Embro

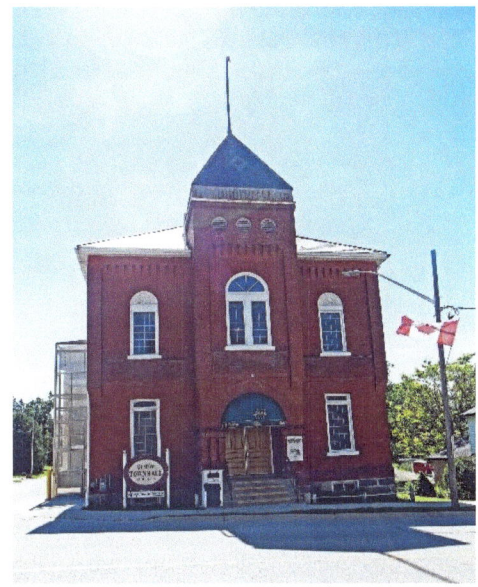

135 Huron Street – Ye Olde Town Hall - 1893

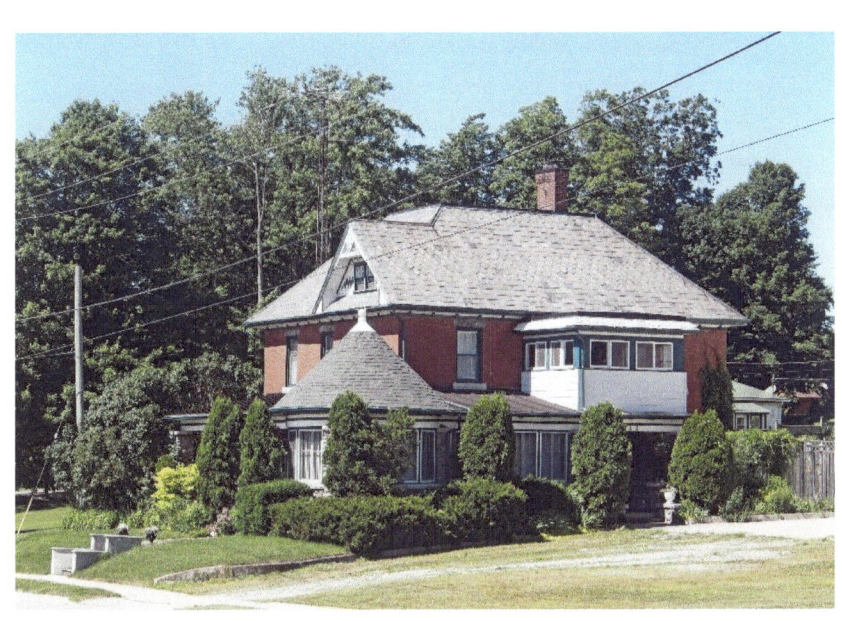

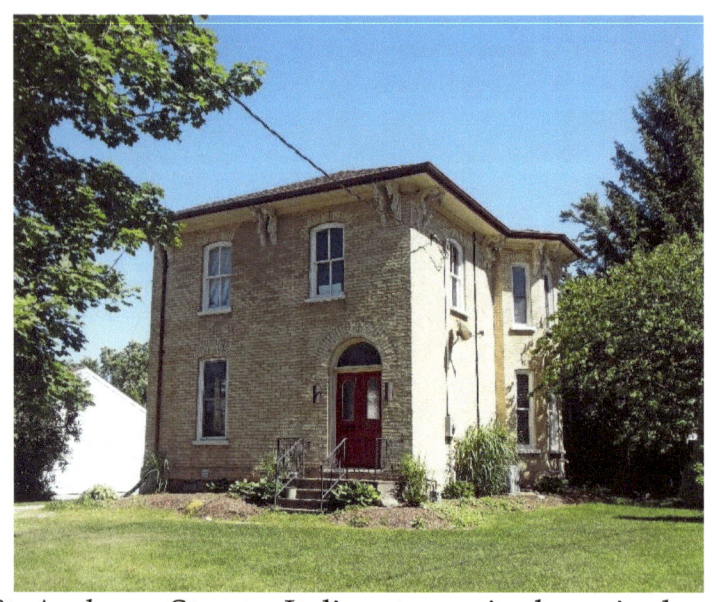

129 St. Andrews Street – Italianate – paired cornice brackets, hipped roof

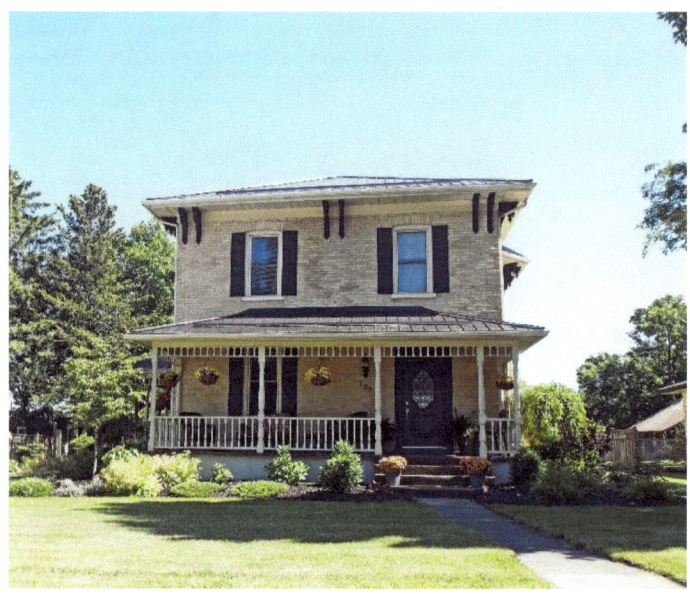

137 St. Andrews Street – hipped roof, cornice brackets

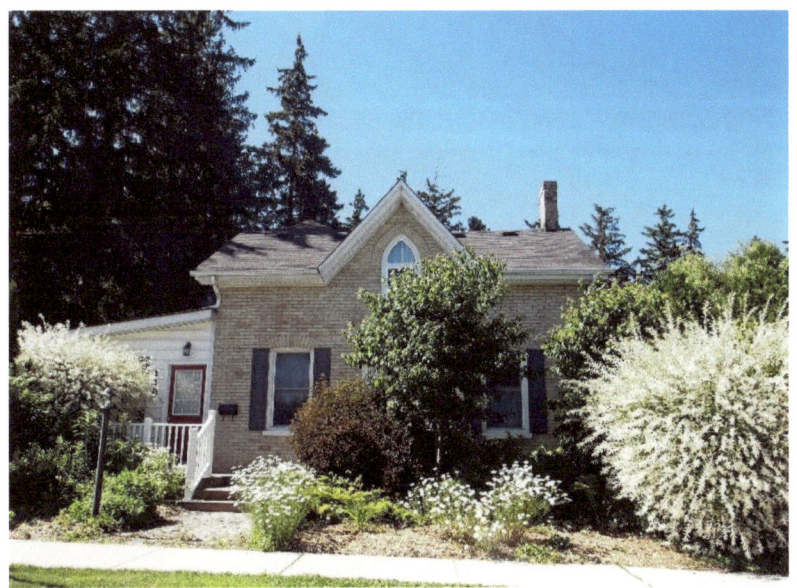

110 St. Andrews Street - Ontario Cottage with center gable

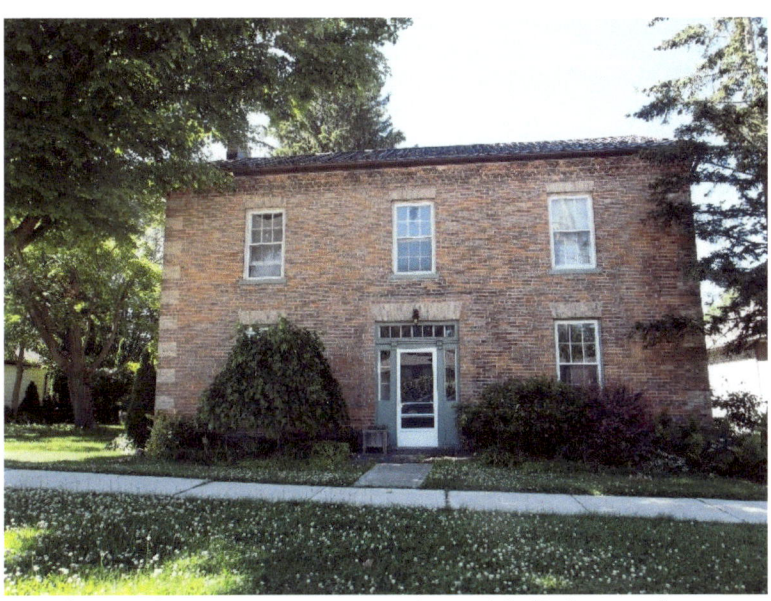

St. Andrews Street – corner quoins, sidelights and transom, voussoirs

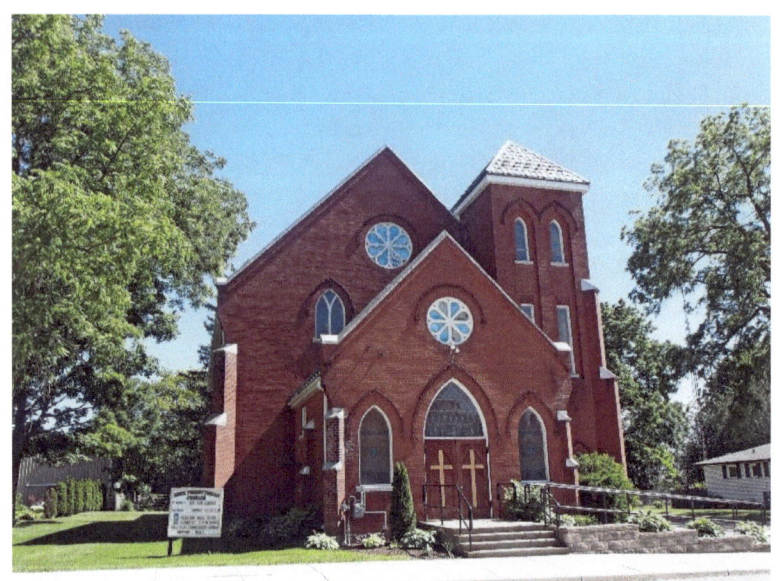

115 St. Andrews Street - Knox Presbyterian Church – 1880 - Gothic Revival – rose windows, three-storey tower, lancet windows, buttresses

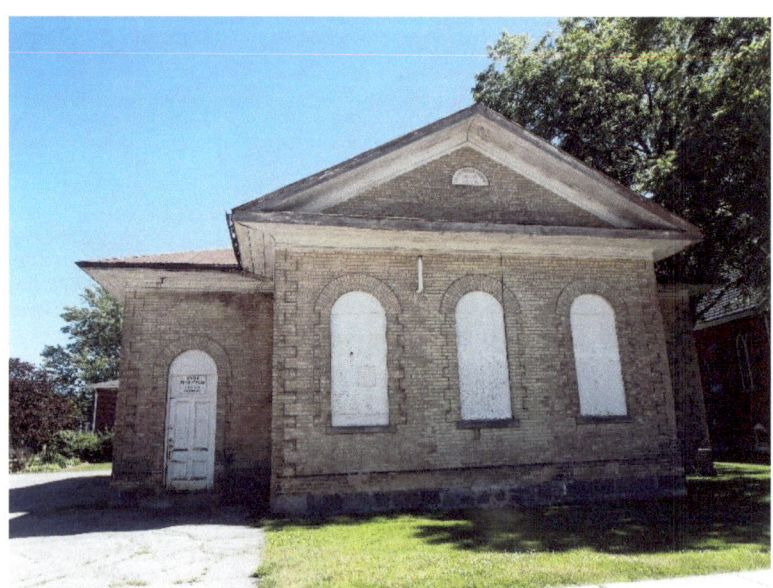

St Andrews Street - Embro Public School erected 1876

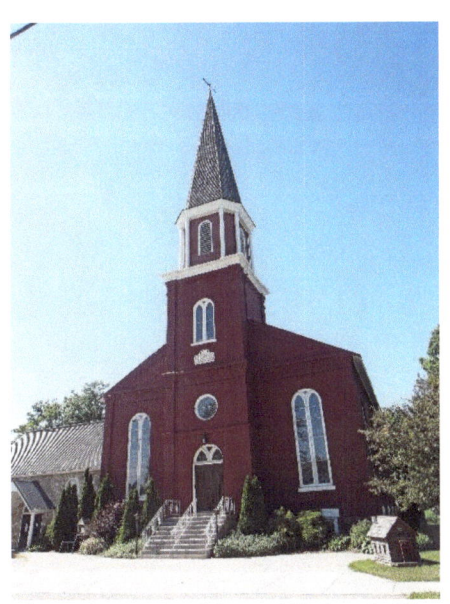

116 Kincardine Street – Knox United Church – 1863

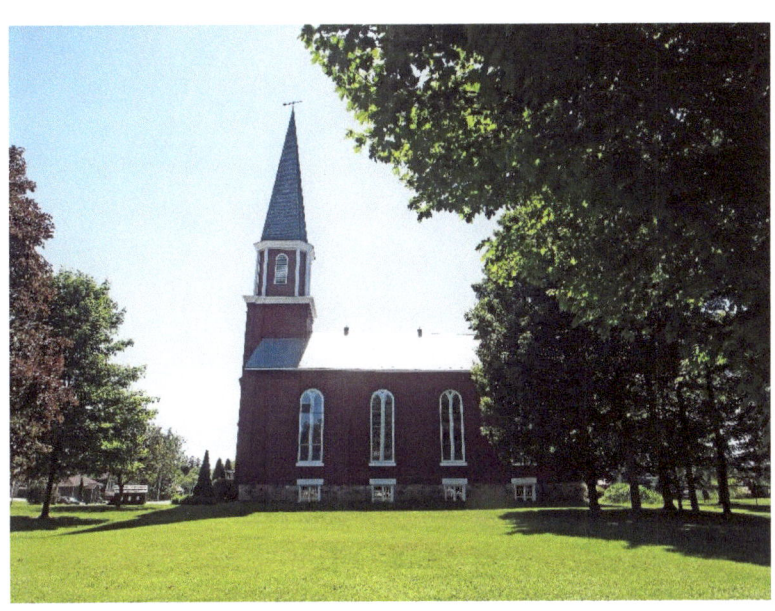

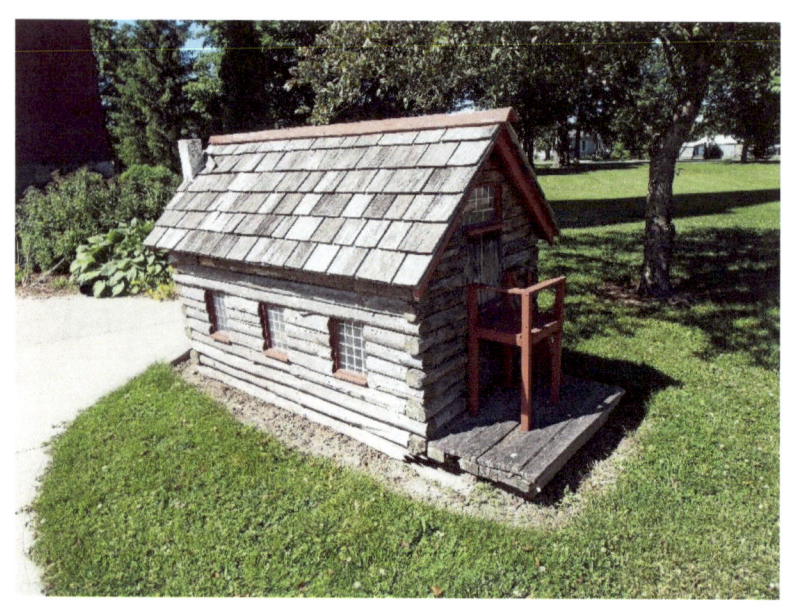

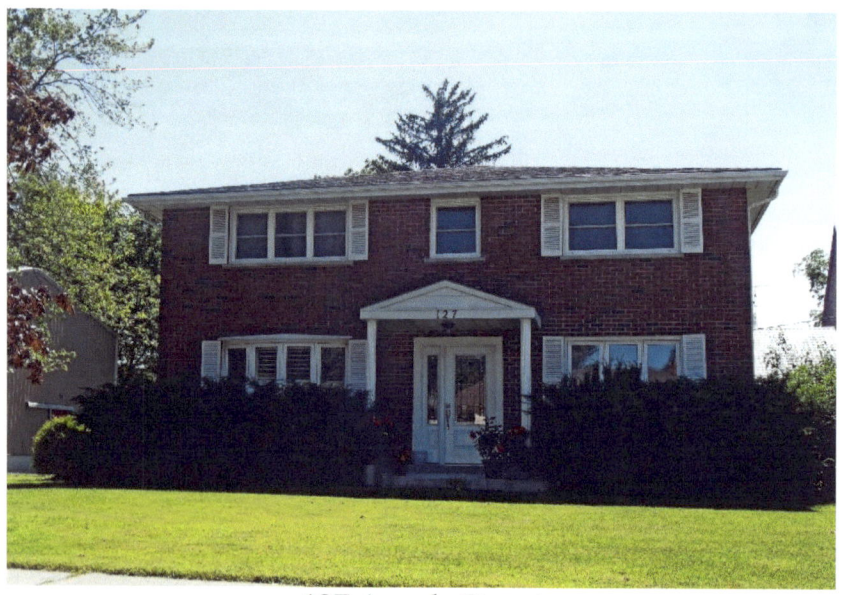

127 Argyle Street

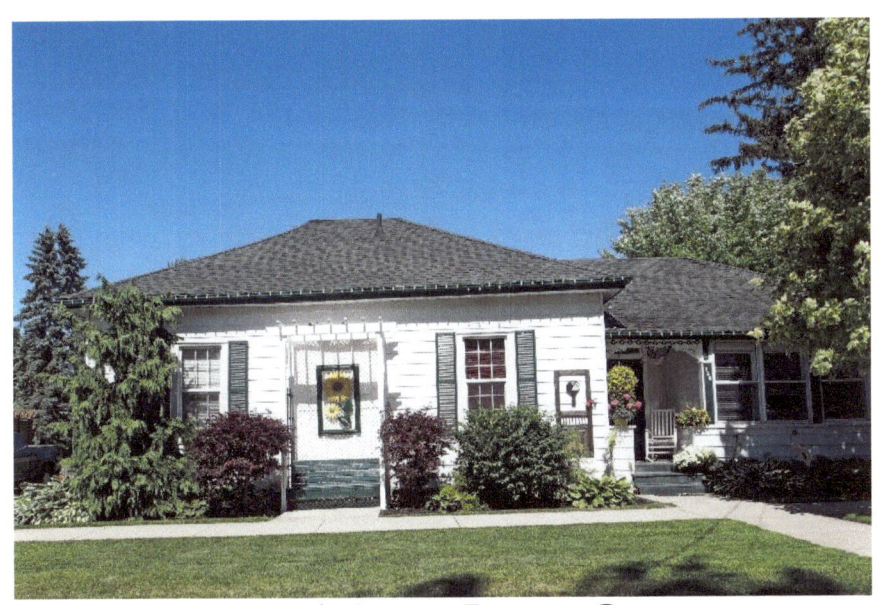
128 Argyle Street – Regency Cottage

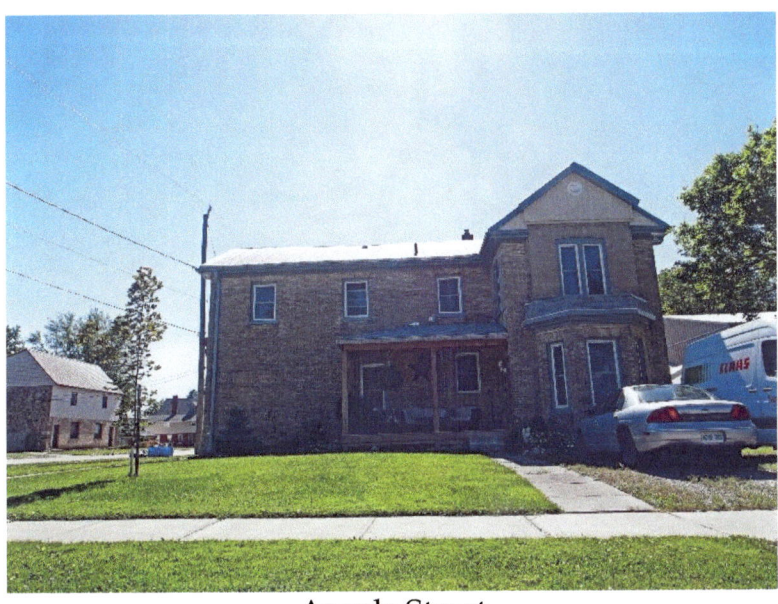
Argyle Street

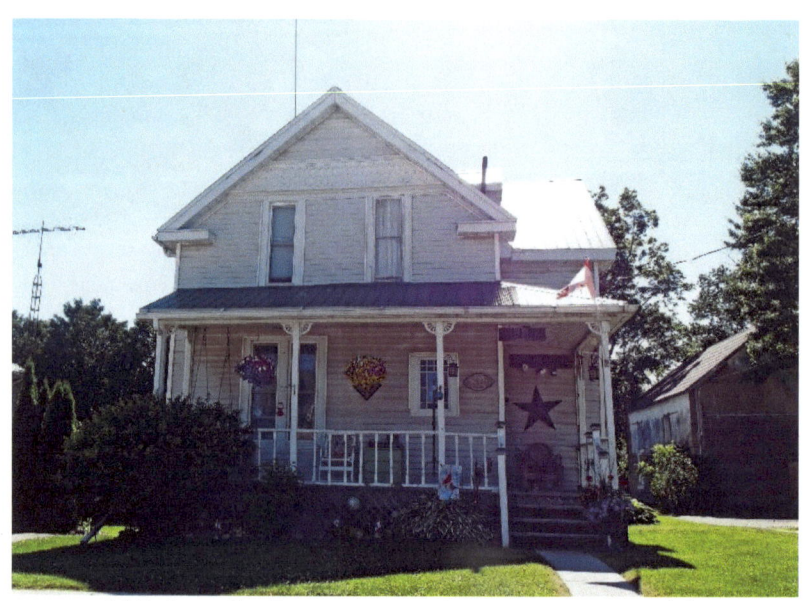

115 Argyle Street – cornice return on gable

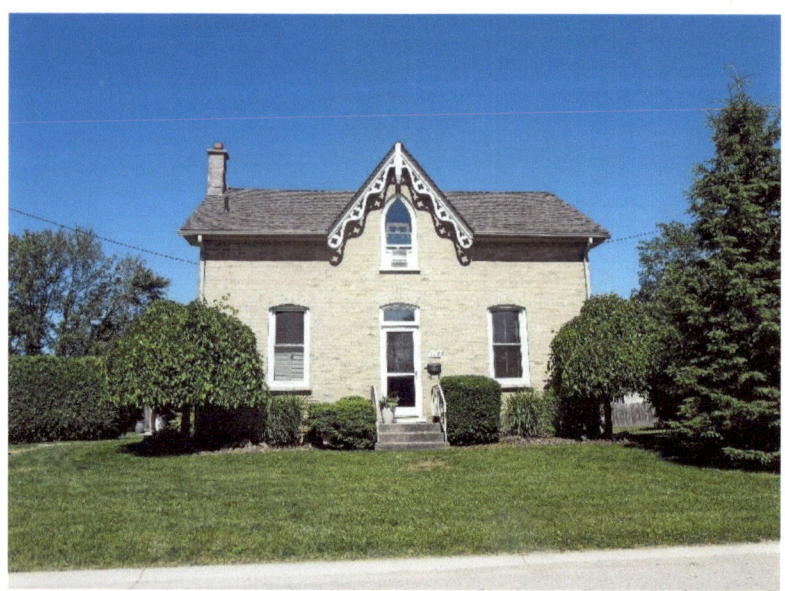

114 Argyle Street – verge board trim and finial on center gable of Ontario Cottage

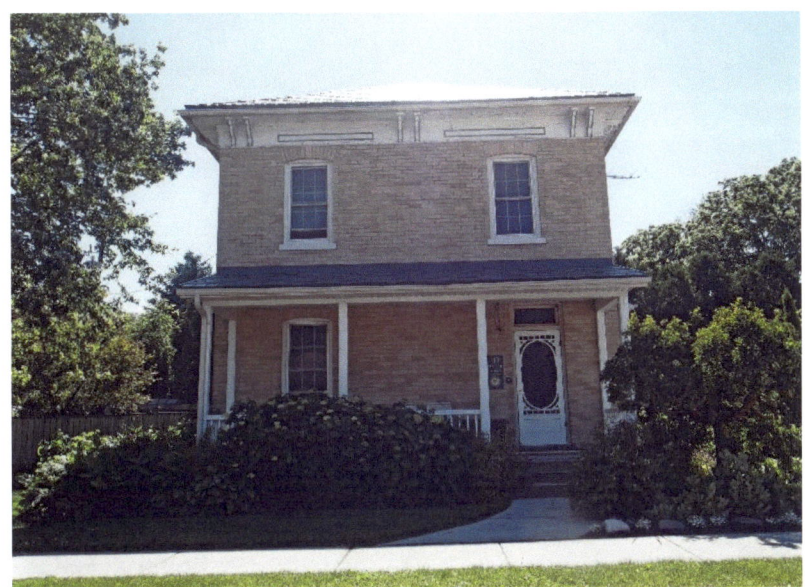

113 Argyle Street – decorative cornice with brackets

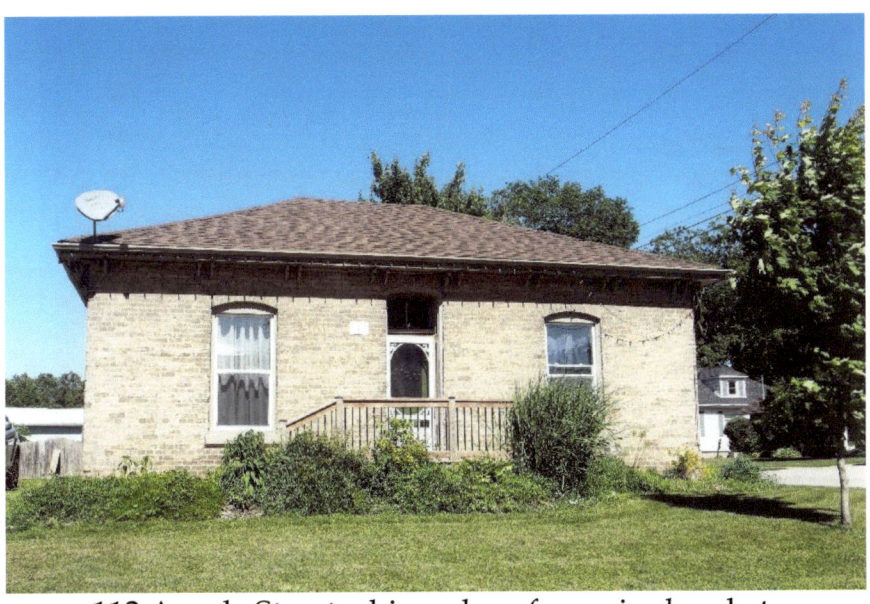

112 Argyle Street – hipped roof, cornice brackets

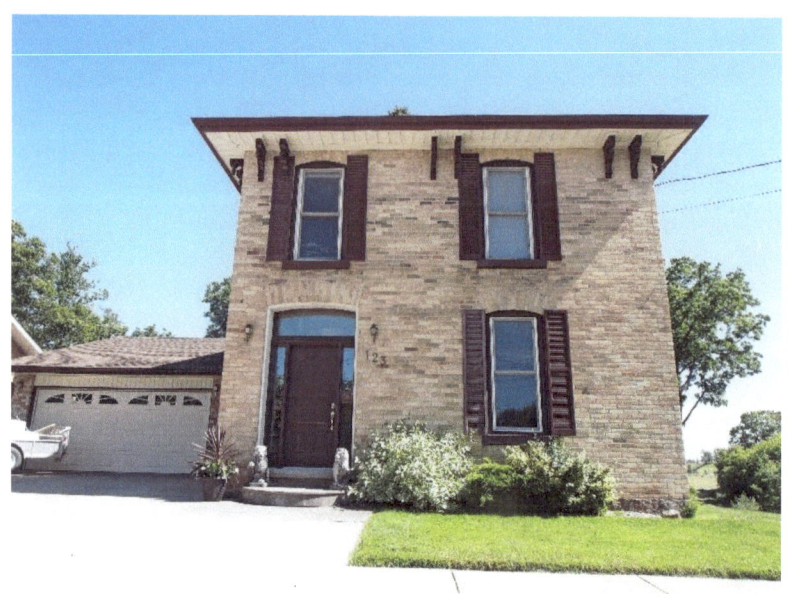

123 John Street – hipped roof, paired cornice brackets, sidelights and transom window

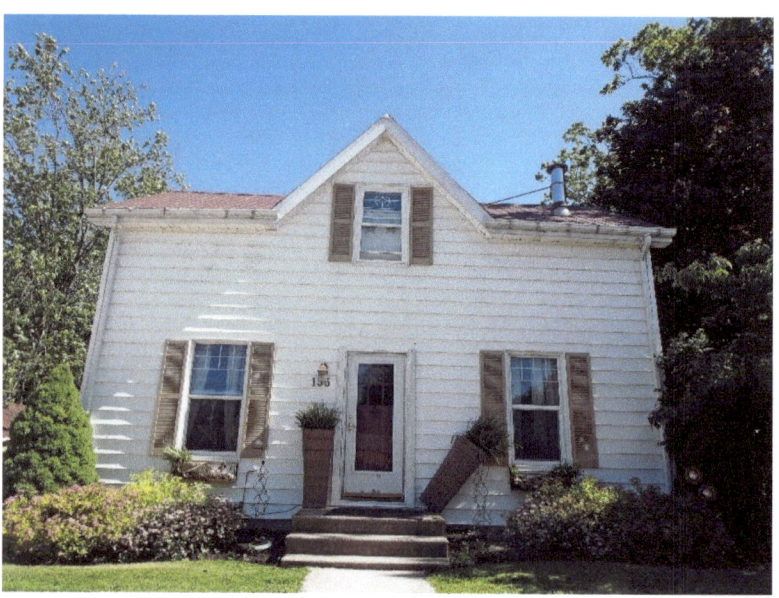

135 John Street

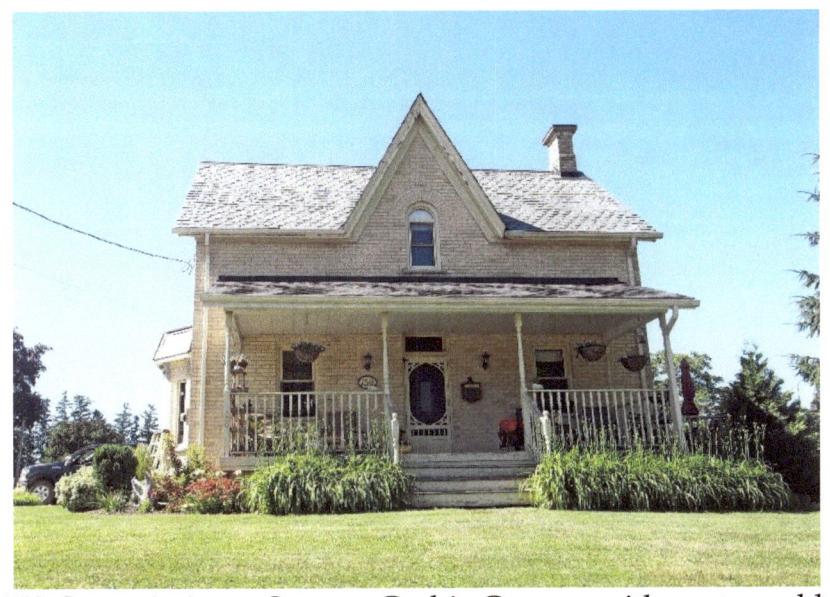

150 Commissioner Street – Gothic Cottage with center gable

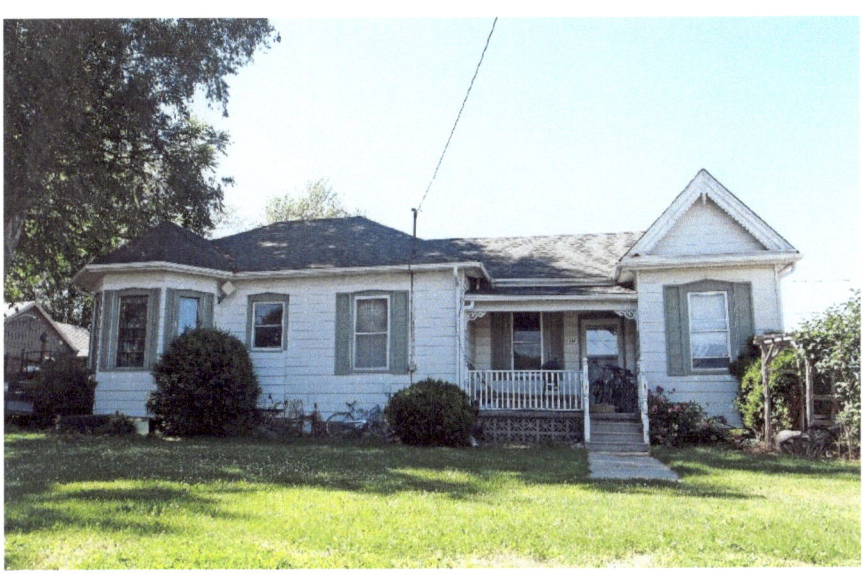

146 Commissioner Street

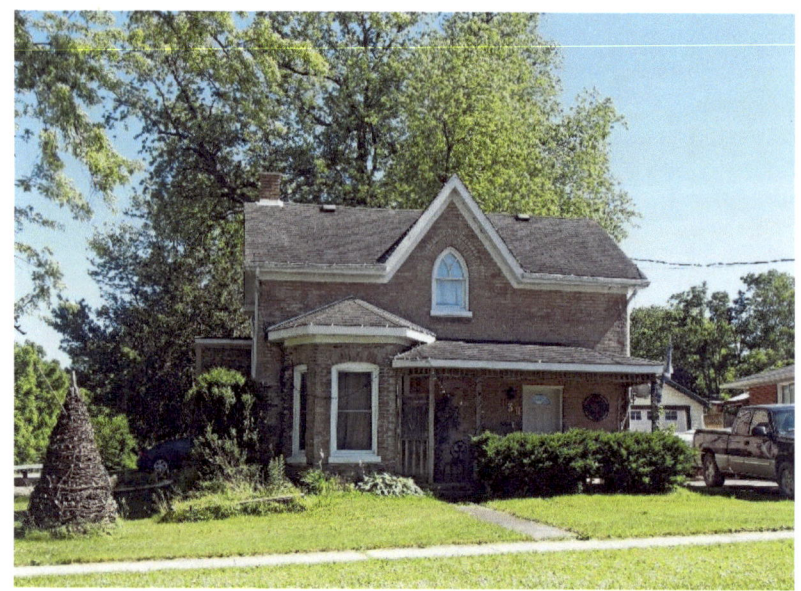

139 Commissioner Street – Ontario Cottage, bay window

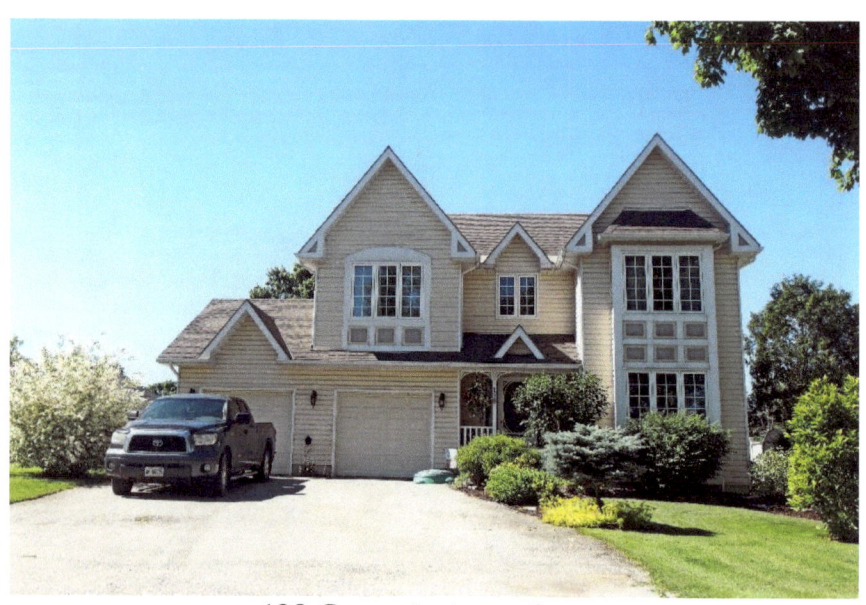

138 Commissioner Street

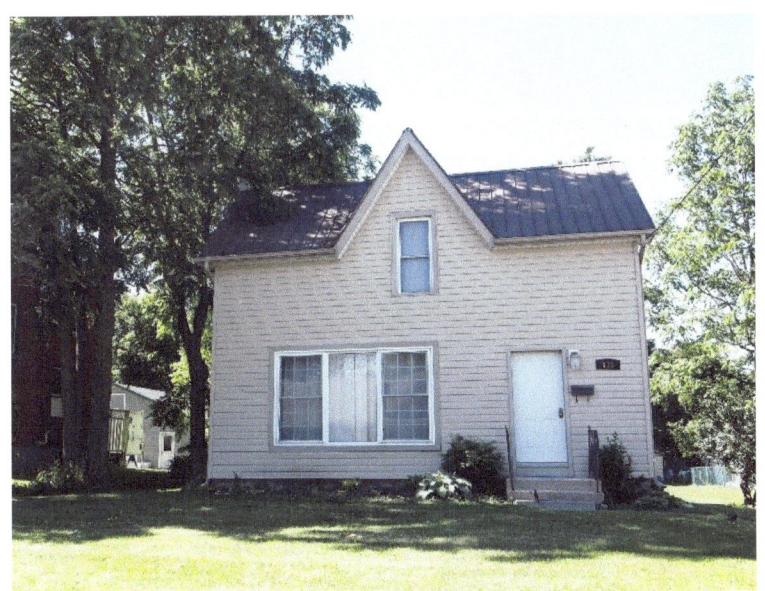

130 Commissioner Street

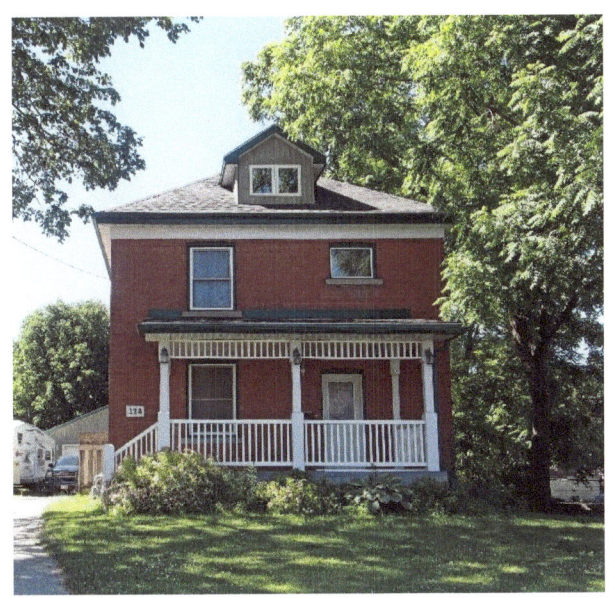

128 Commissioner Street – dormer

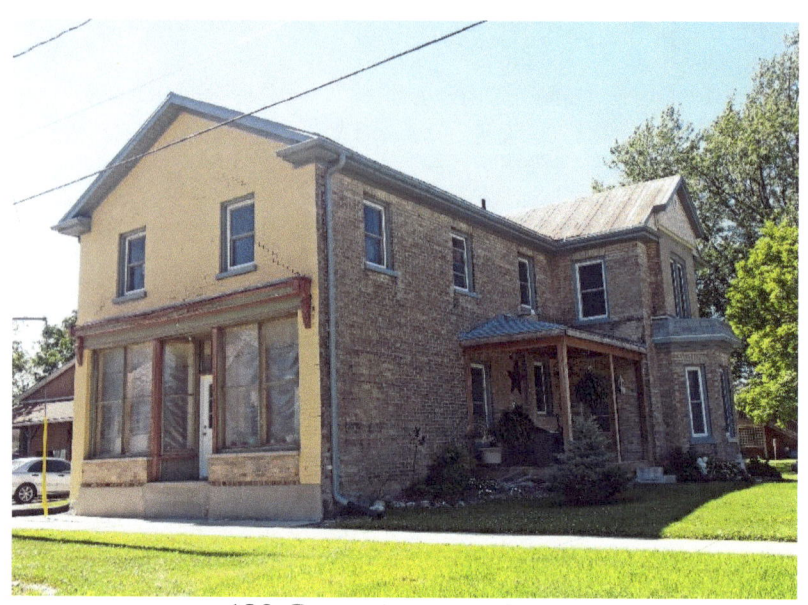
120 Commissioner Street

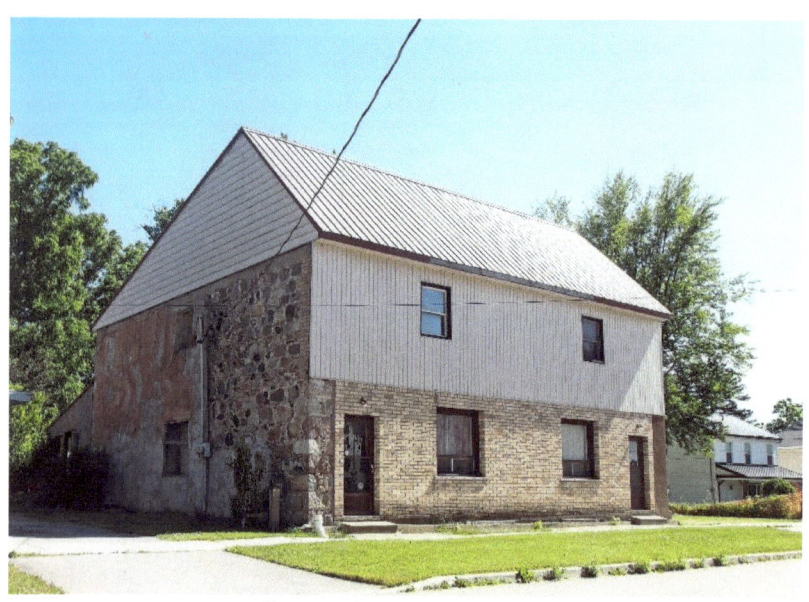
Commissioner Street

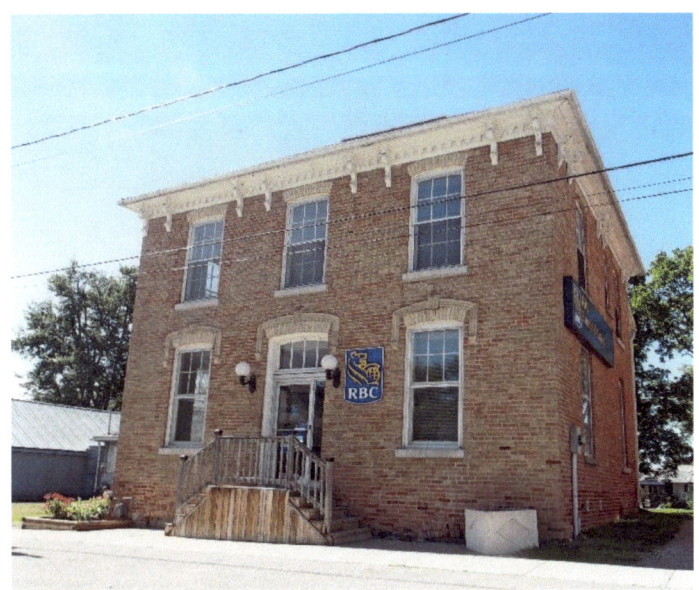

112 Commissioner Street – cornice brackets

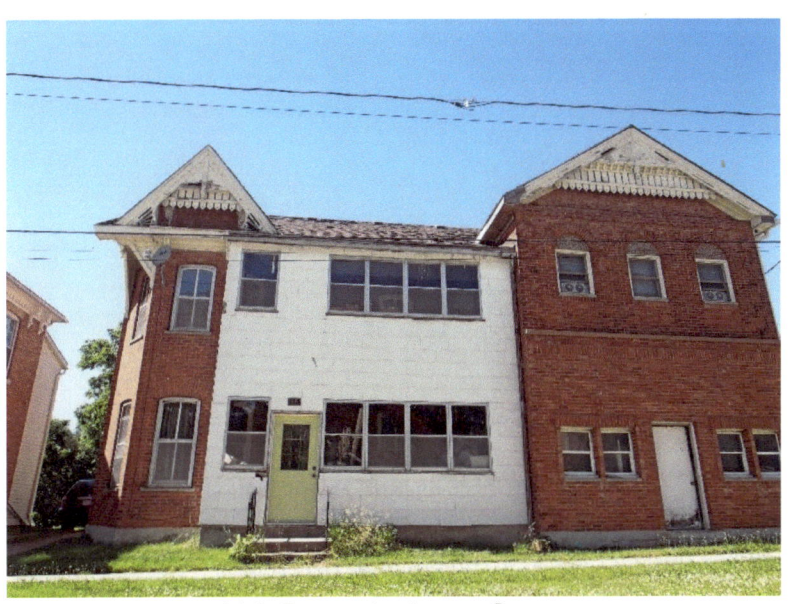

114 Commissioner Street

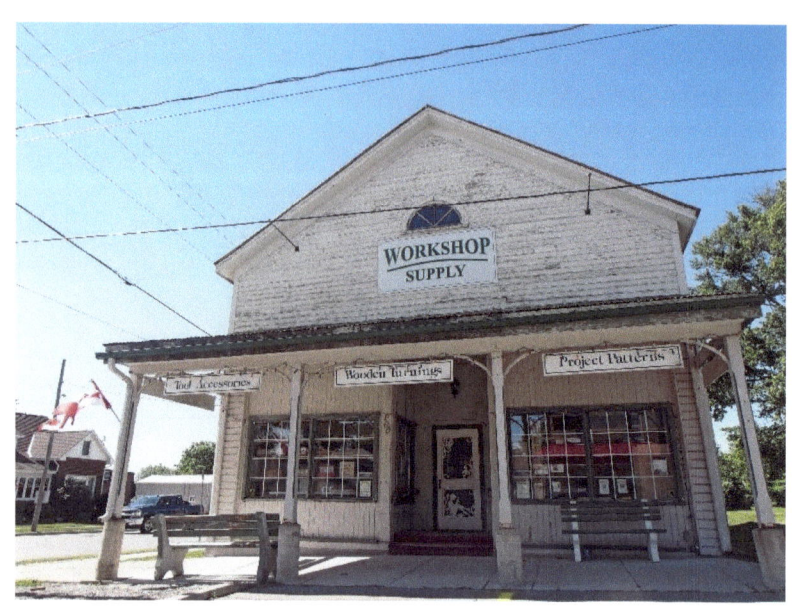

100 Commissioner Street

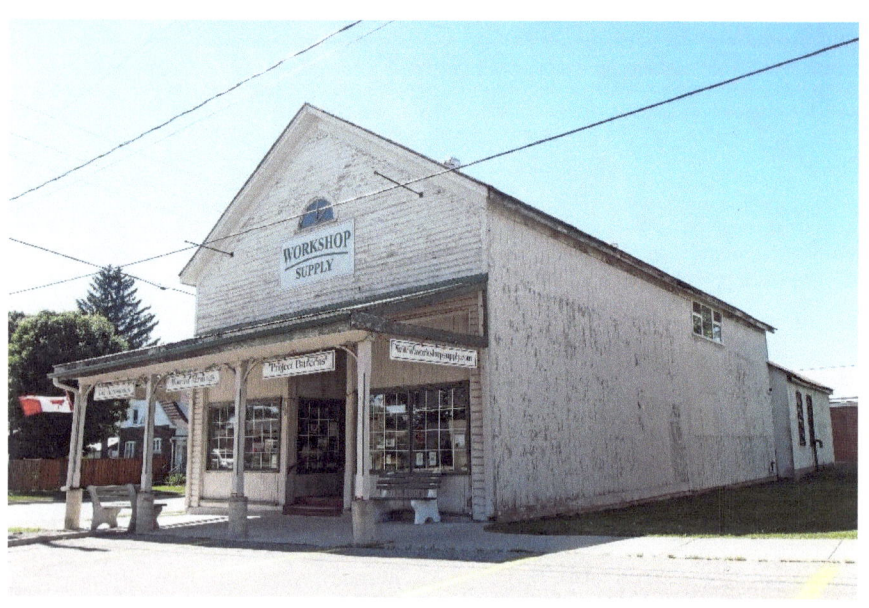

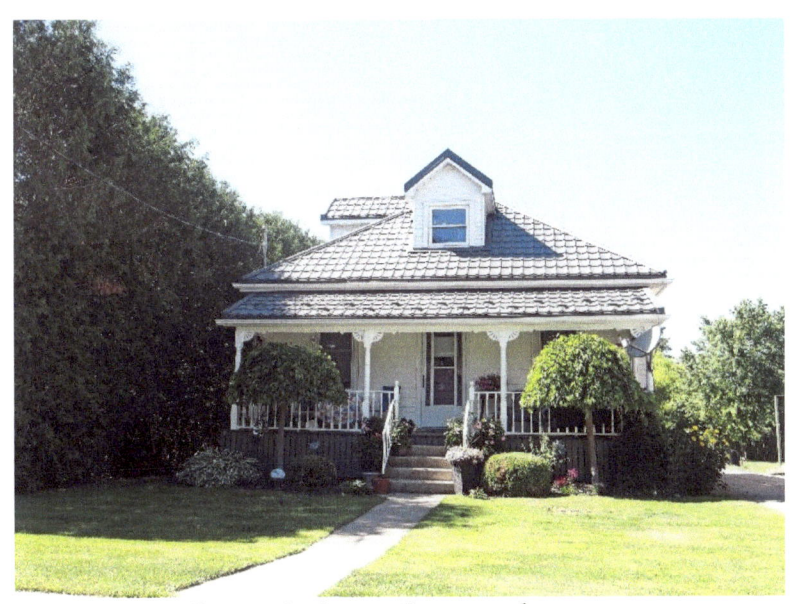

Commissioner Street - dormer

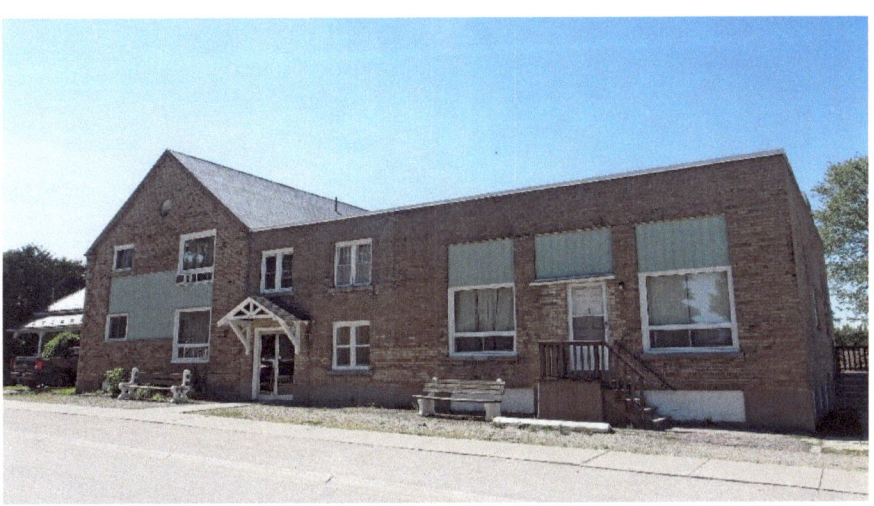

86 Commissioner Street – Embro Continuation School 1926-1931

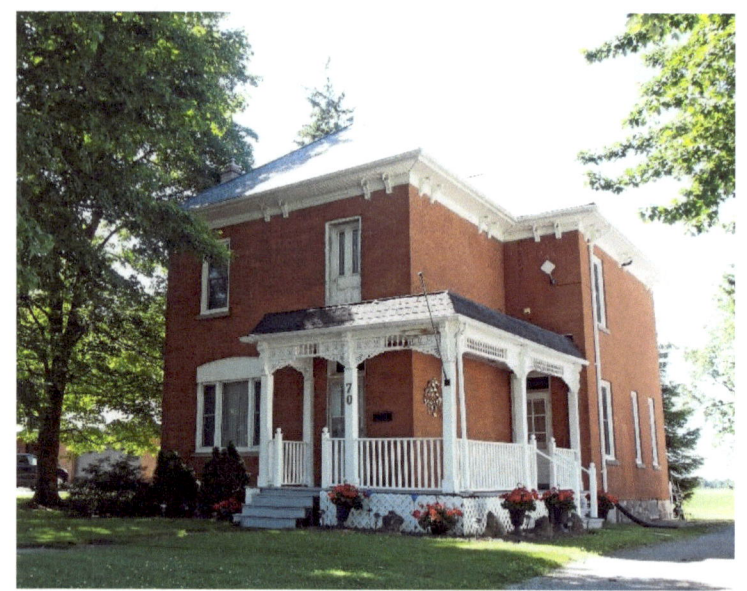

70 Commissioner Street – hipped roof, cornice brackets

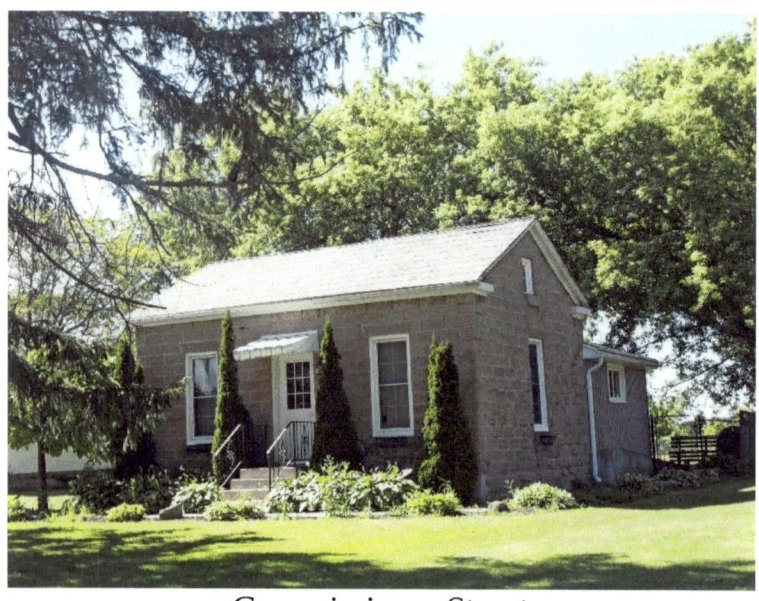

Commissioner Street

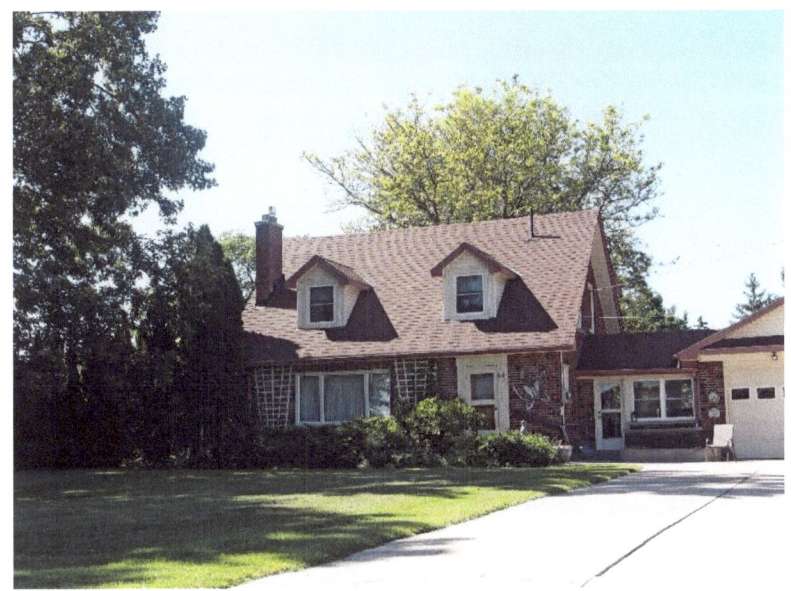
64 Commissioner Street - dormers

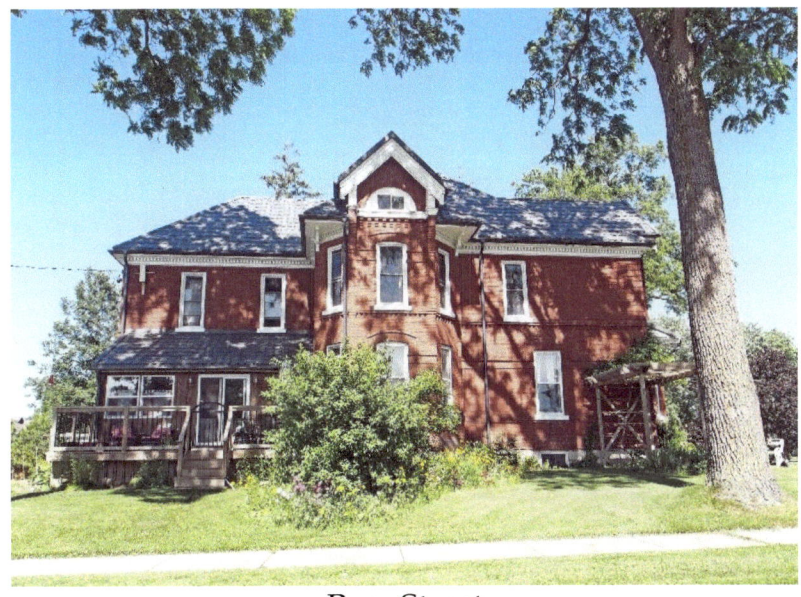
Ross Street

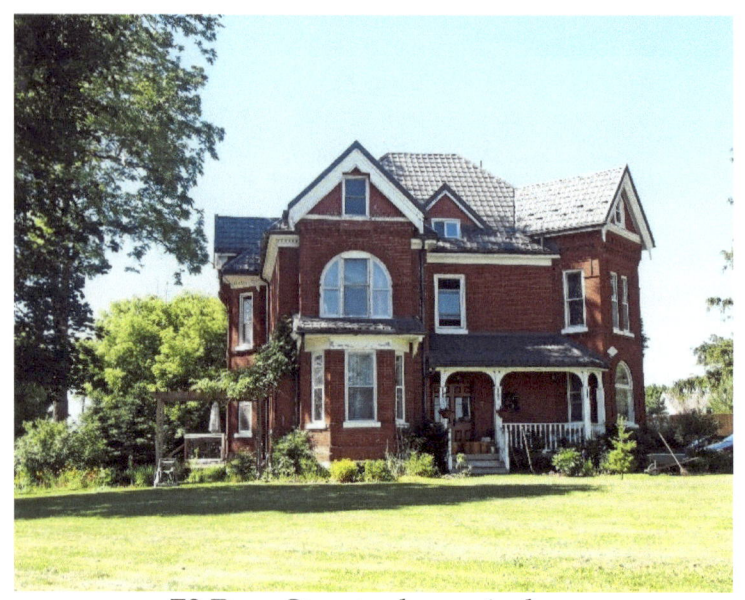

70 Ross Street – bay window

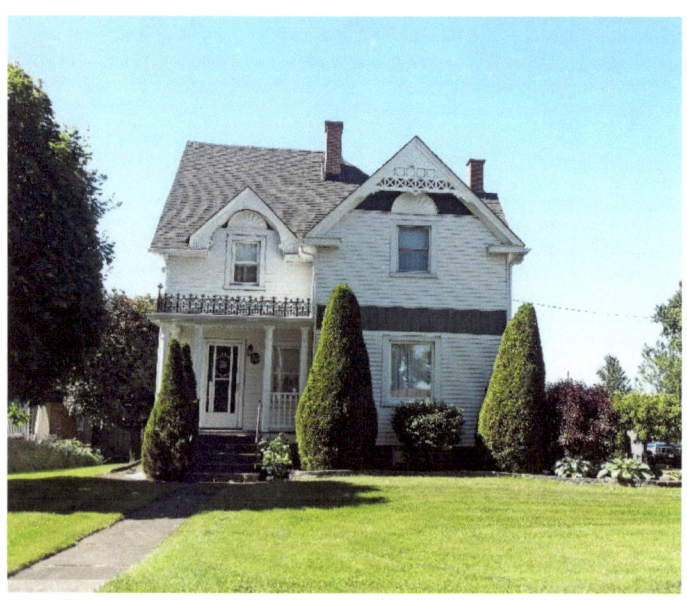

76 Ross Street – iron cresting above porch, trim on gable

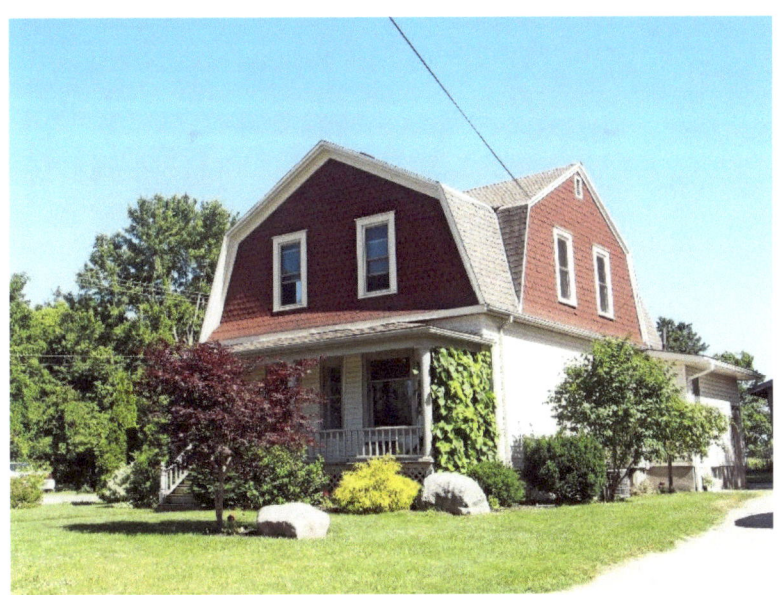

87 Ross Street – Neo-Colonial – gambrel roofs

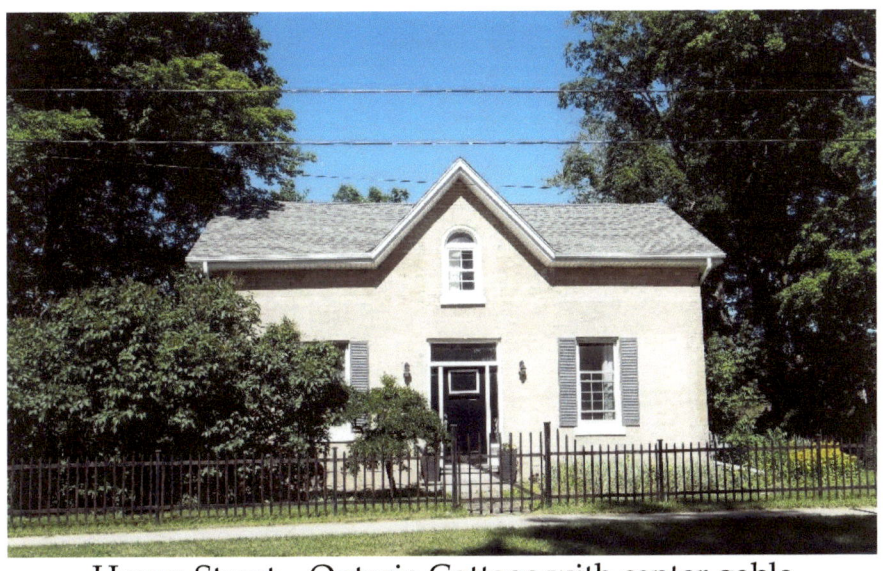

Huron Street – Ontario Cottage with center gable

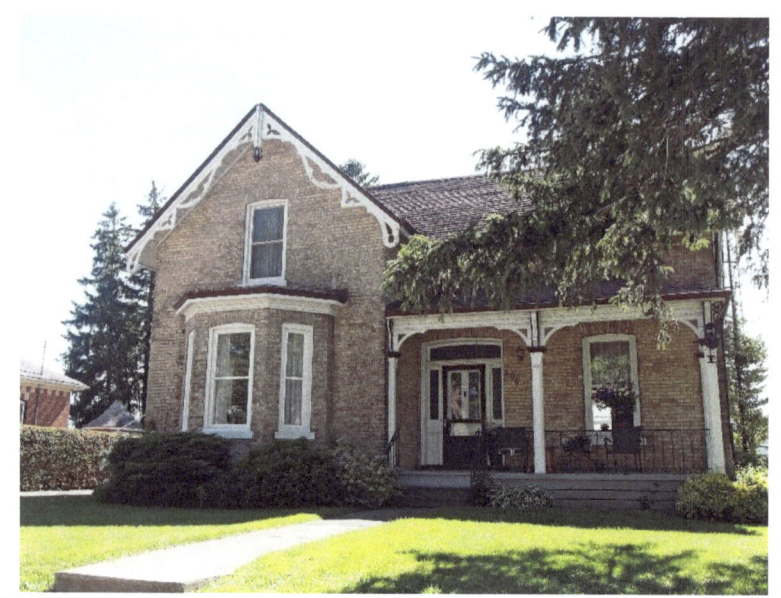

109 Huron Street – Gothic Revival – verge board trim on gable, bay window

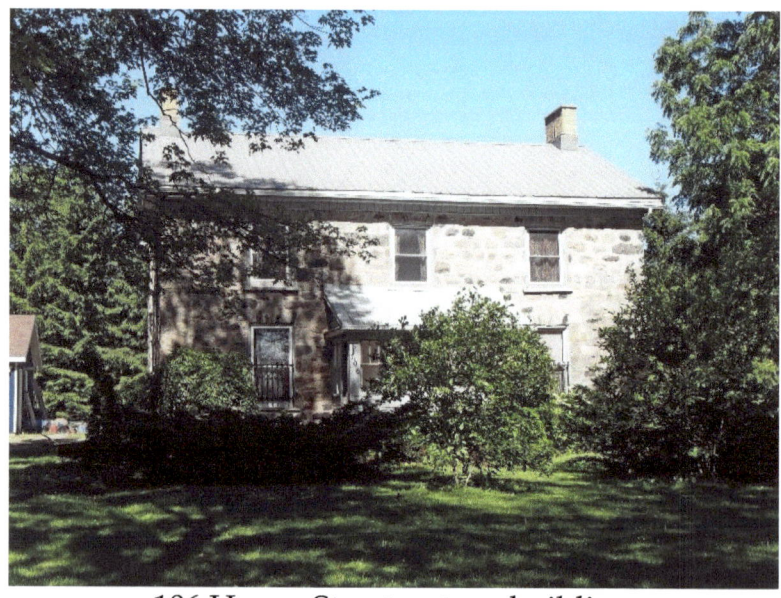

106 Huron Street – stone building

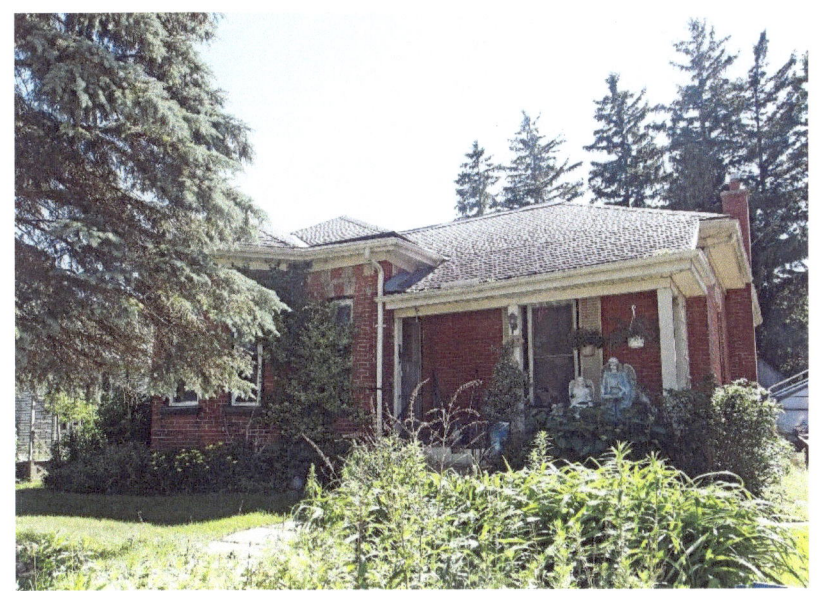

107 Huron Street

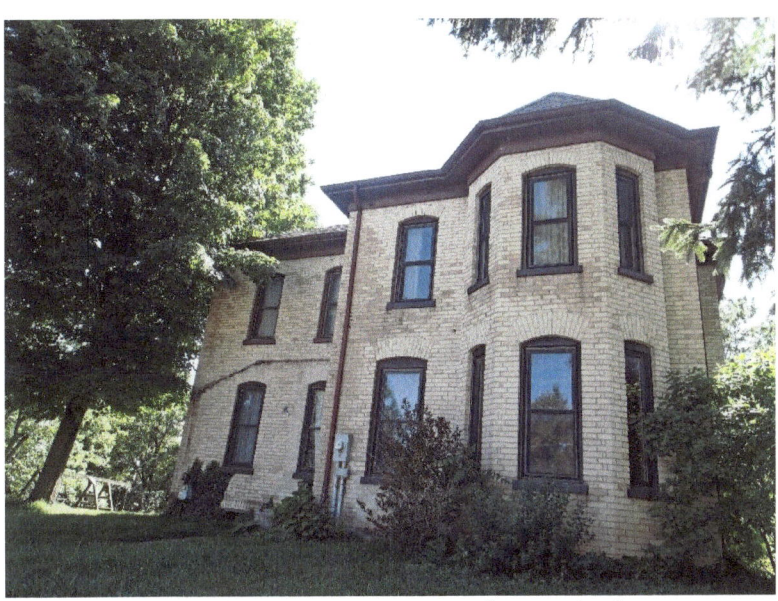

Huron Street - two-storey bay window

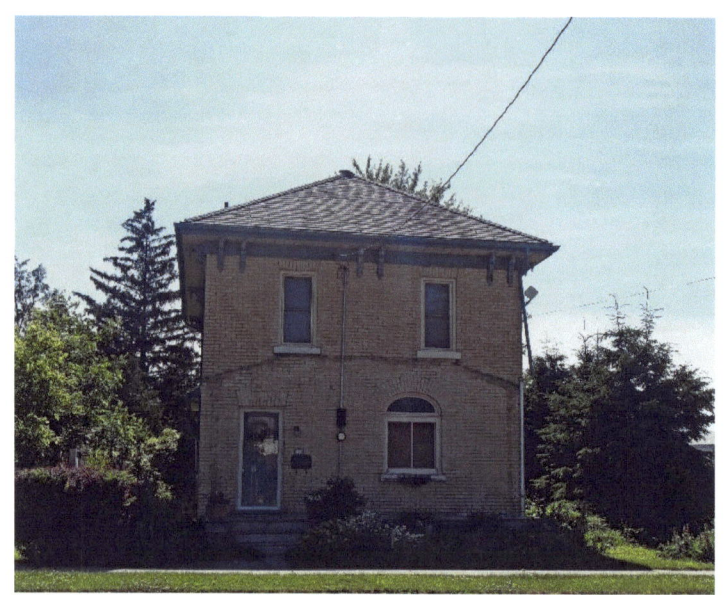
115 Huron Street

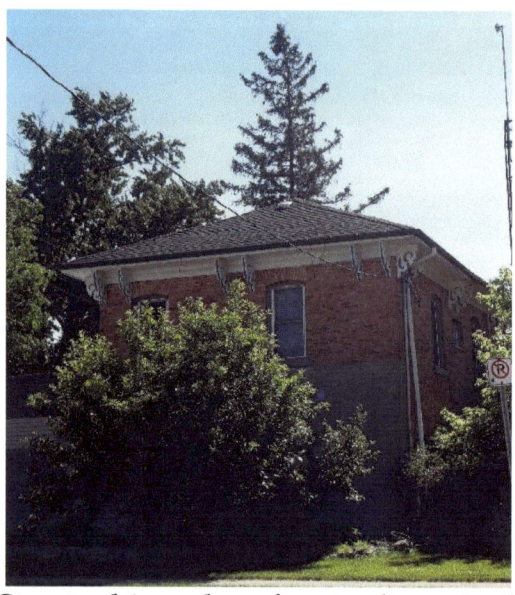
Huron Street – hipped roof, paired cornice brackets

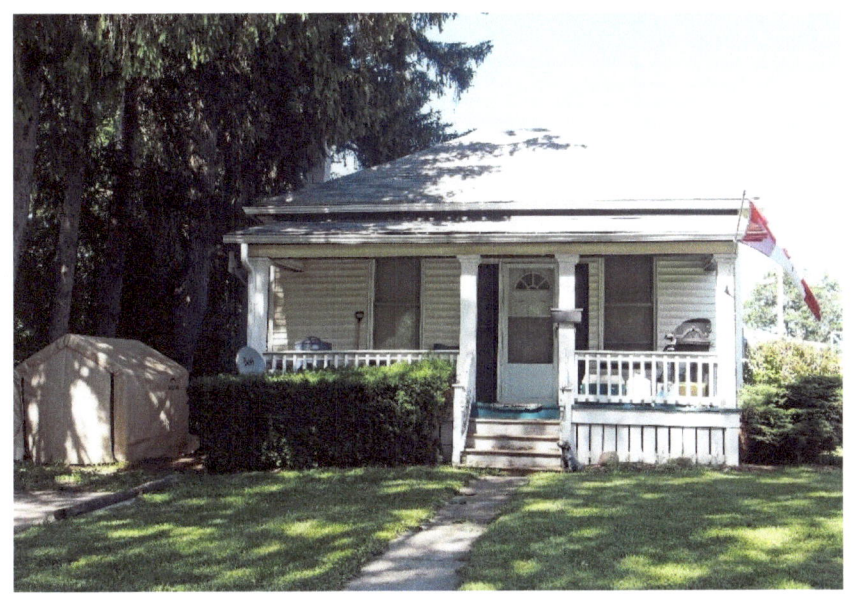

130 Elgin Street – Regency Cottage

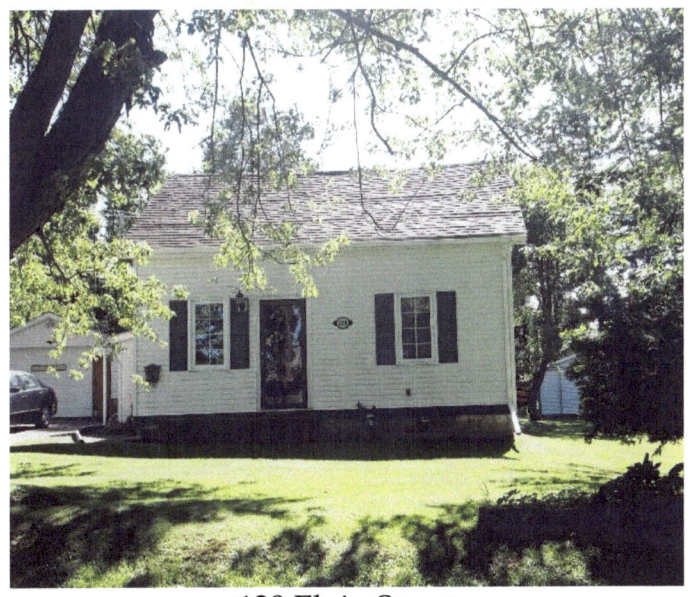

129 Elgin Street

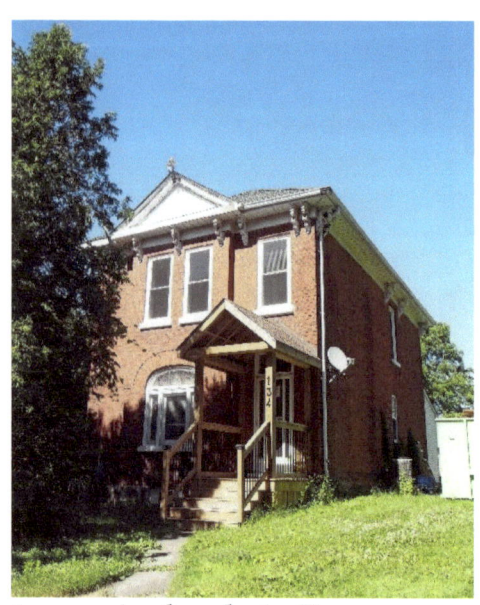

134 Elgin Street – cornice brackets, Romanesque style window arch on lower level, pediment

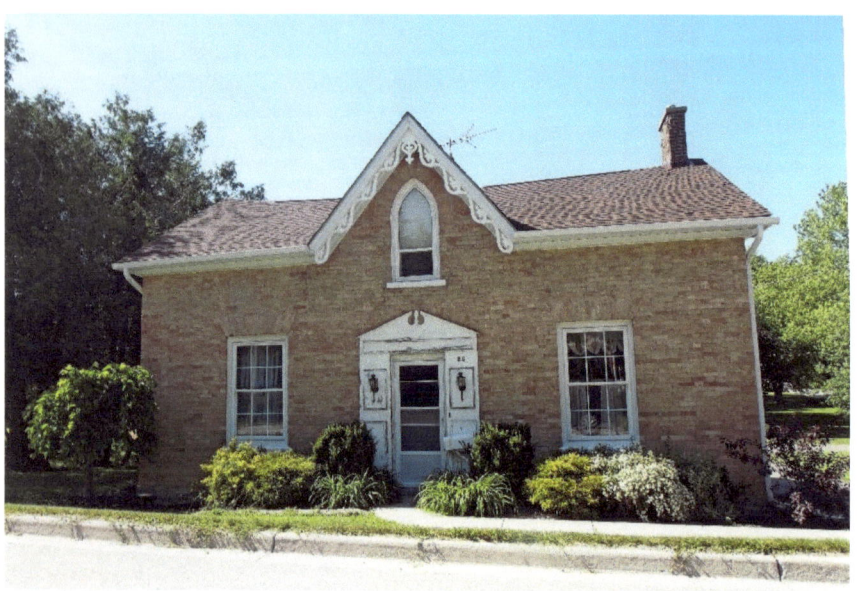

86 Union Street – Ontario Cottage with verge board trim on center gable

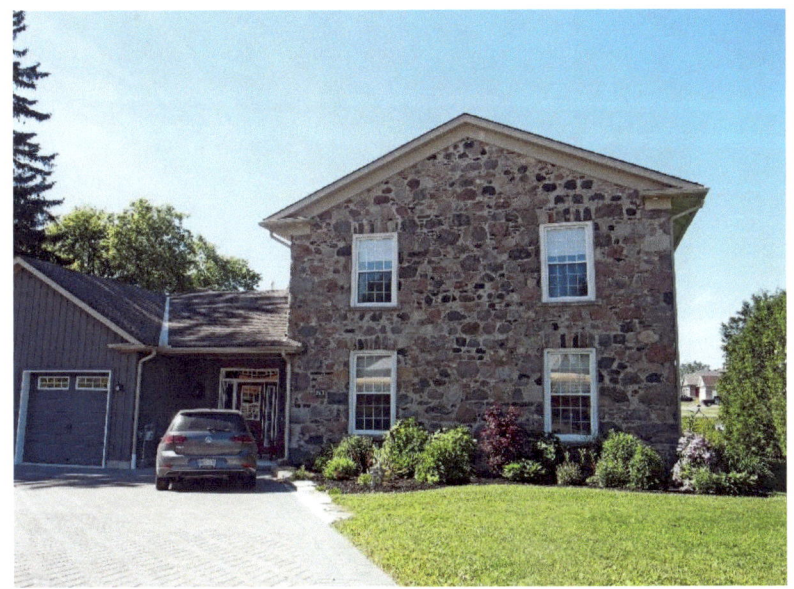

74 Union Street – field stone

Medina

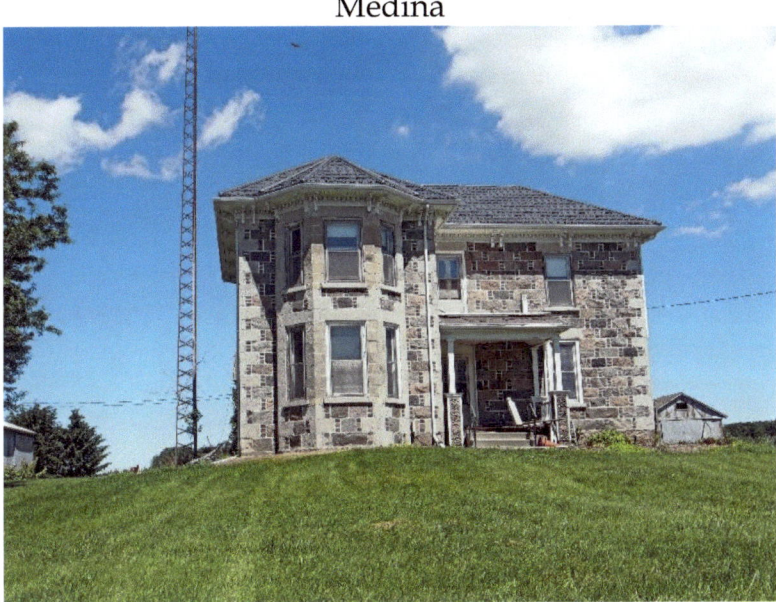

Field stone, two-storey bay window, corner quoins, cornice brackets

Lakeside

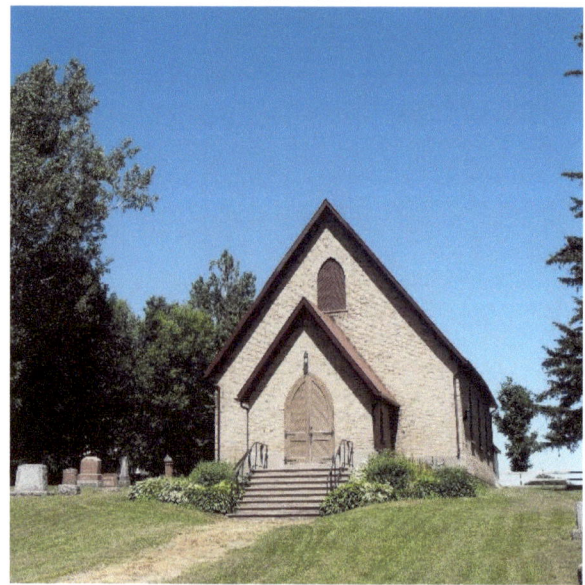

256554 Sunova Crescent - Christ Church Anglican – built in 1863

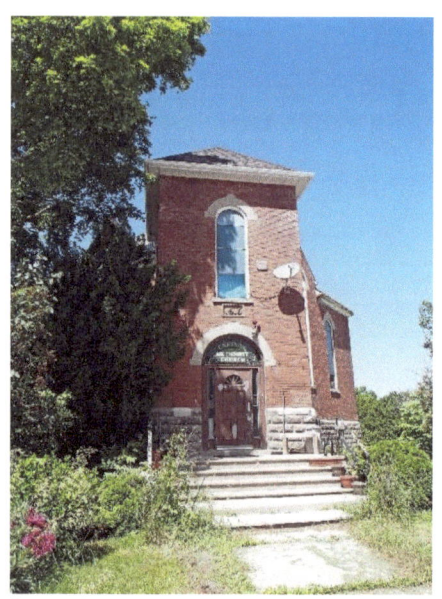

Lakeside Methodist Church – 1915

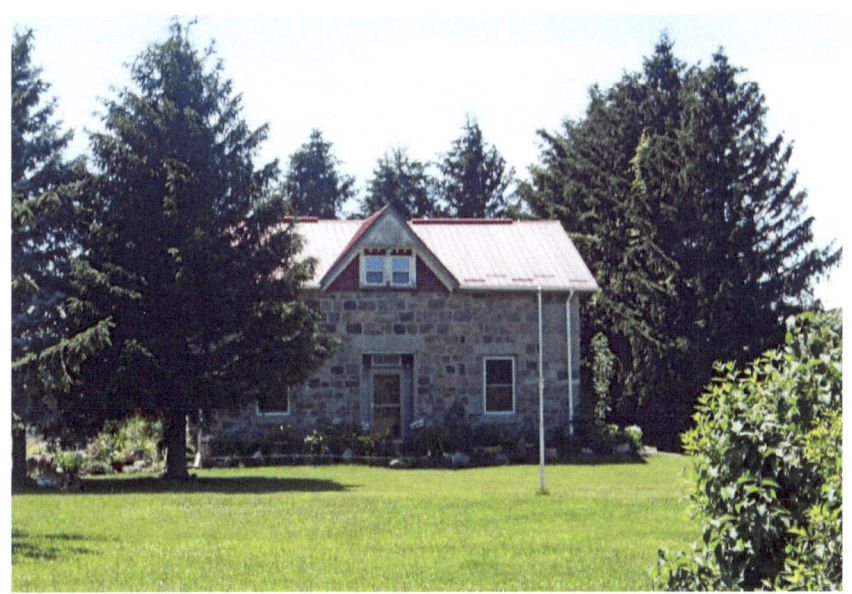

Field stone

Uniondale

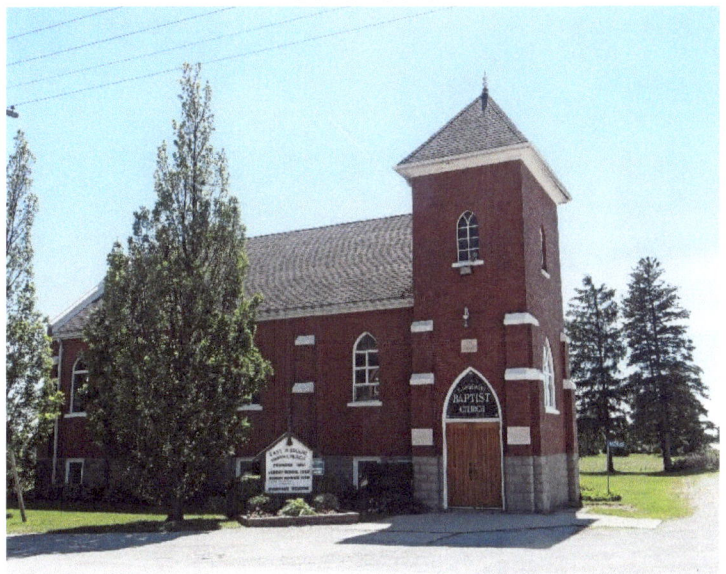

East Nissouri Baptist Church – rebuilt 1926

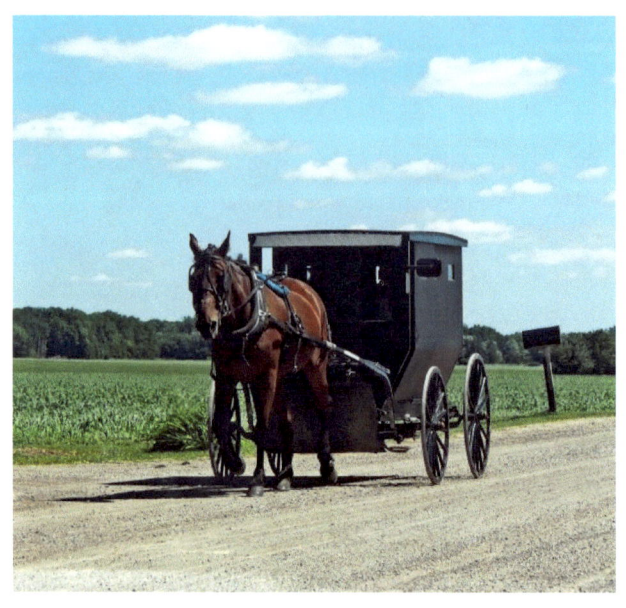

Mennonite horse-drawn buggy

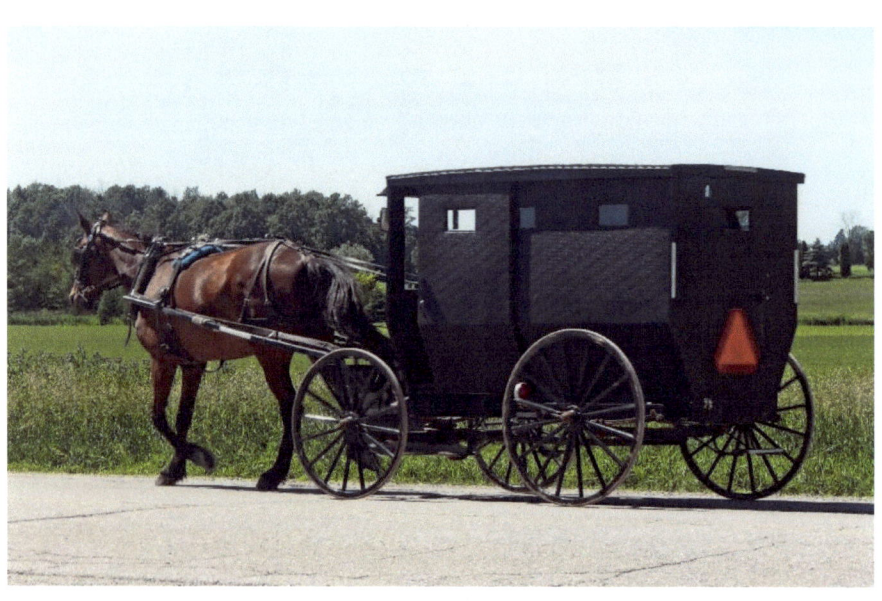

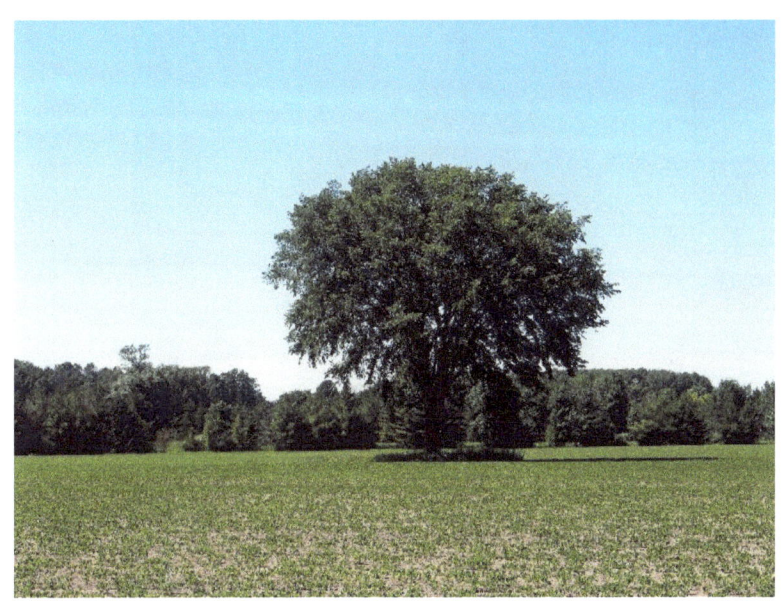

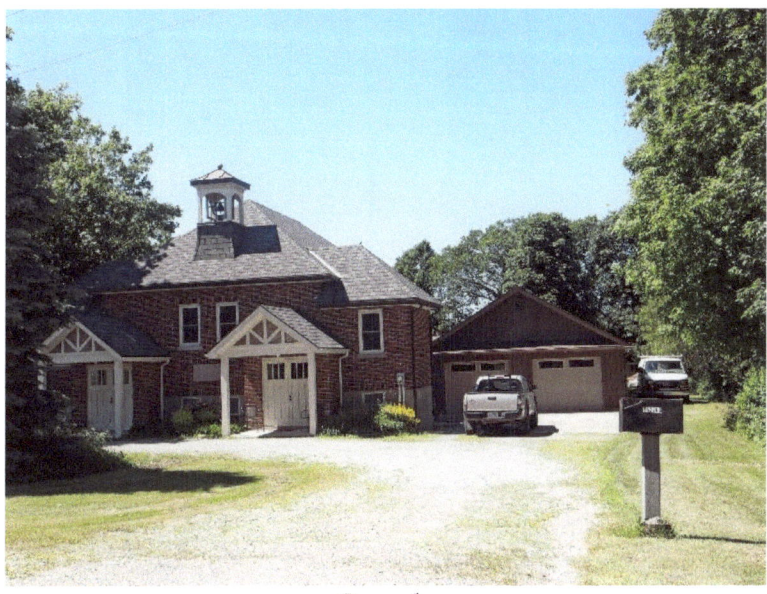

Cupola

Harrington

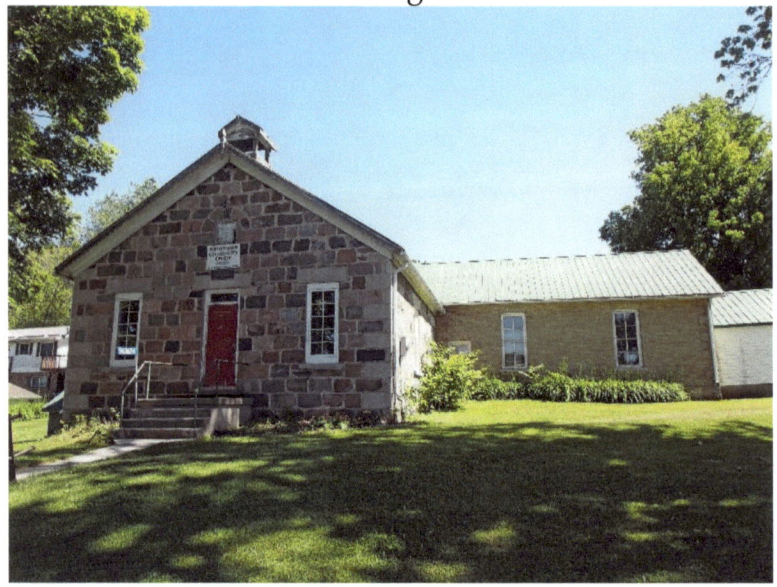

Harrington Community Centre – field stone, cupola

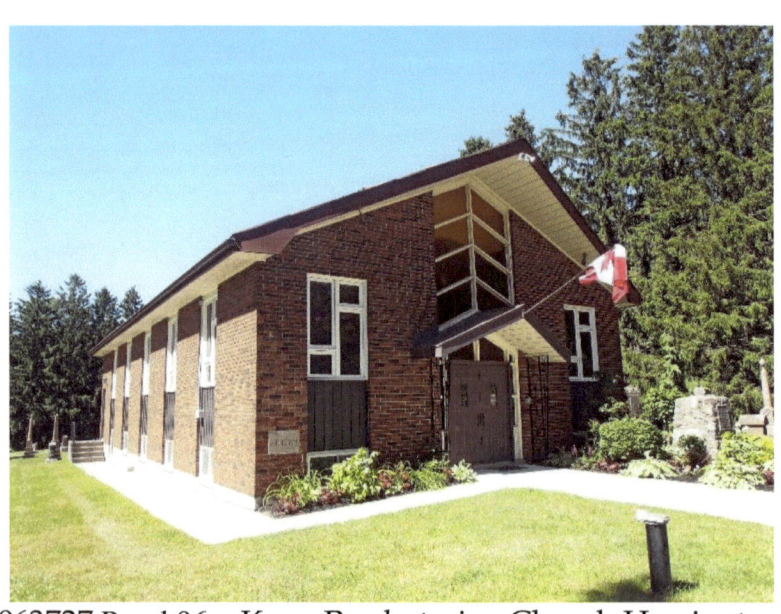

#963727 Road 96 – Knox Presbyterian Church Harrington – rebuilt in 1964 after it burned down

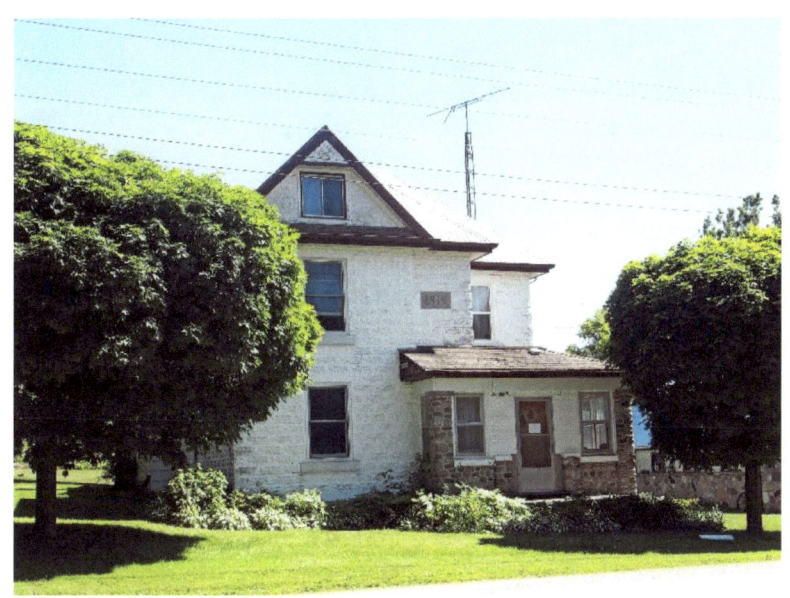

c. 1914

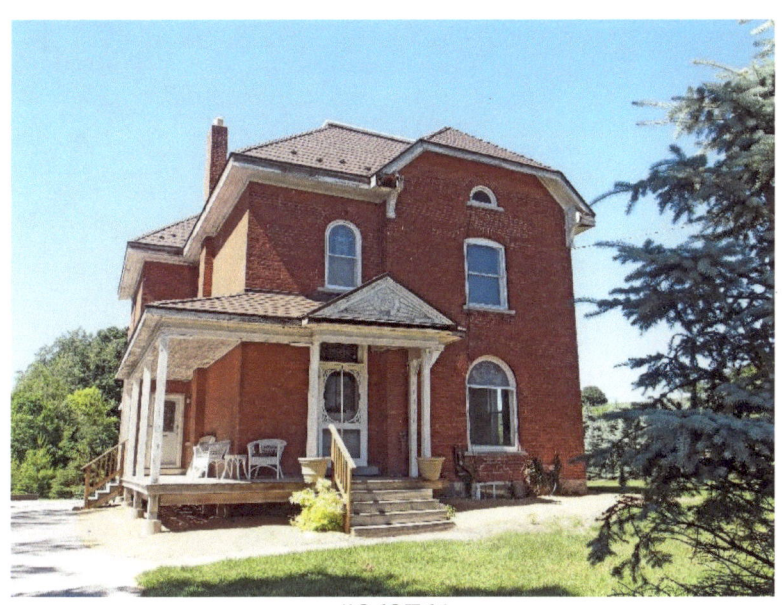

#963761

Kintore

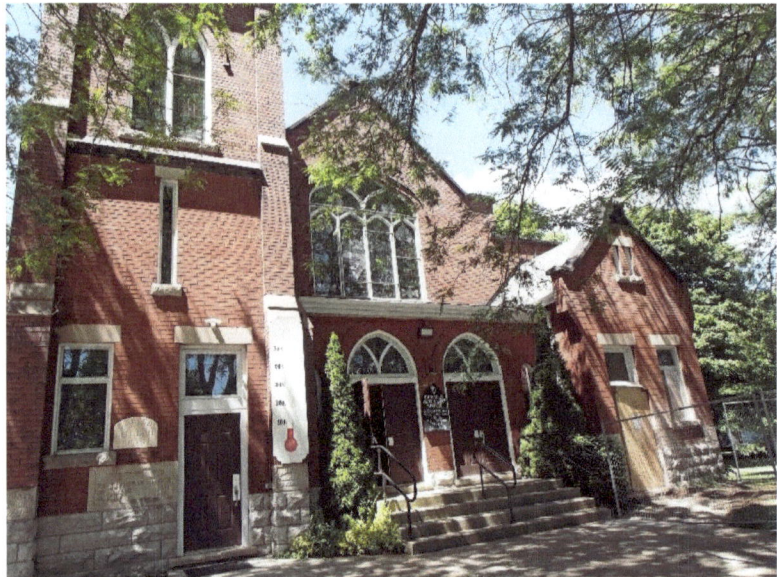

Presbyterian Church – A.D. 1871, rebuilt 1914 – now Chalmers United Church Kintore – battlementing on tower

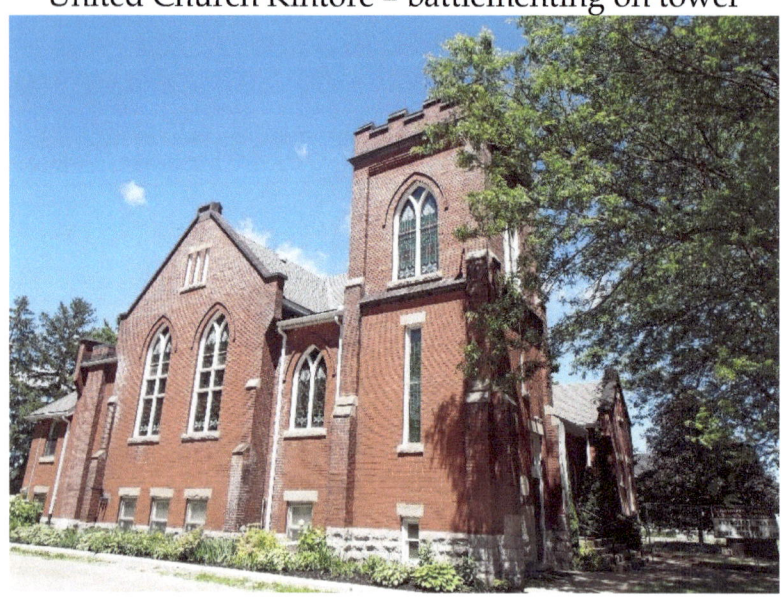

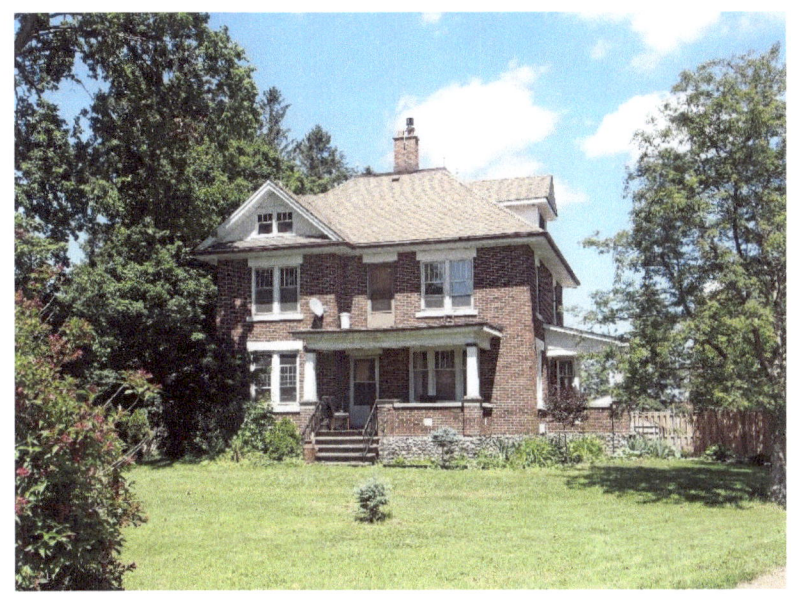

195962

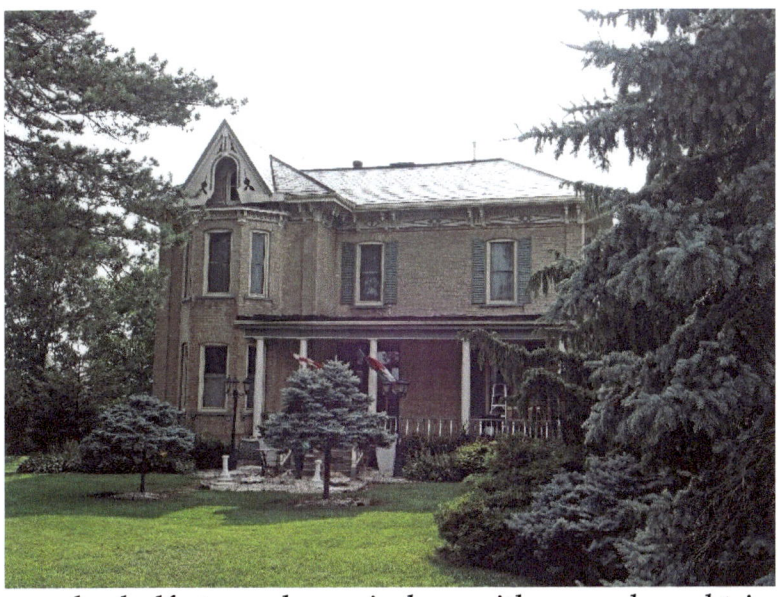

Two-and-a-half-storey bay window with verge board trim on gable, decorative cornice with brackets

Thamesford

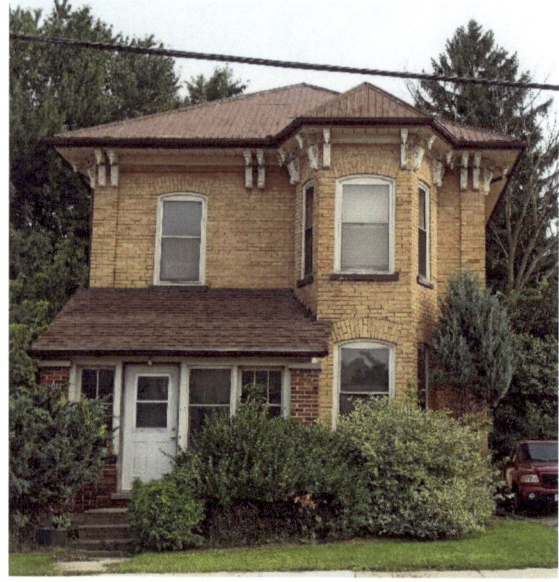

109 Dundas Street

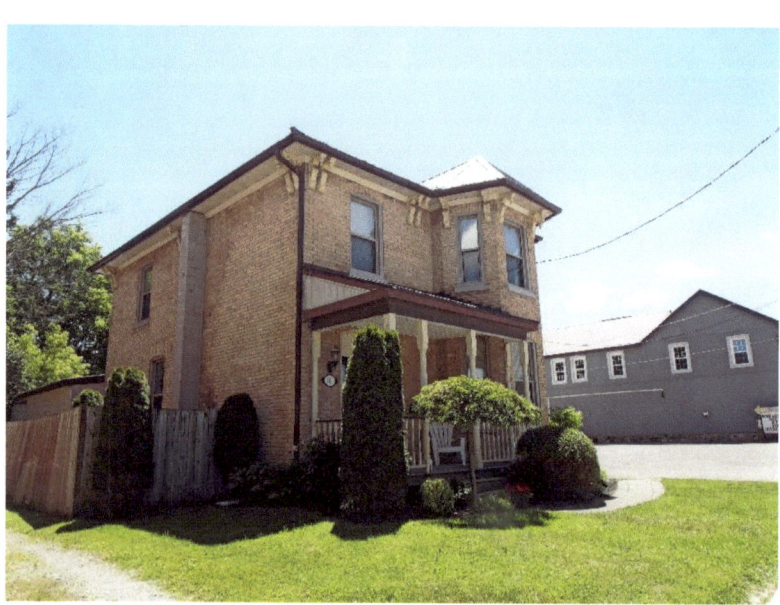

113 Dundas Street – cornice brackets, two-storey bay window

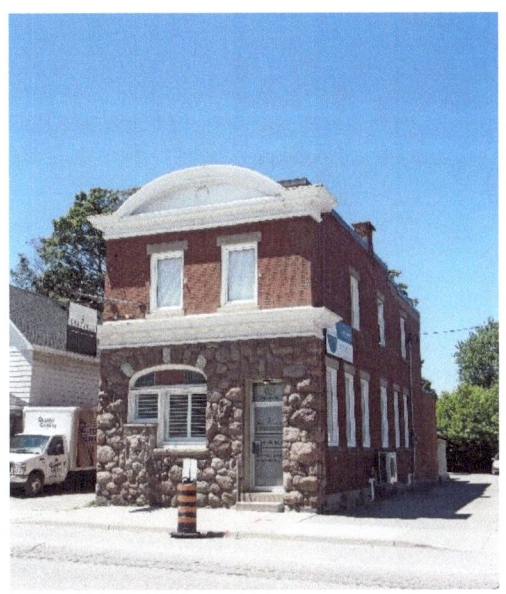

132 Dundas Street - cobblestone

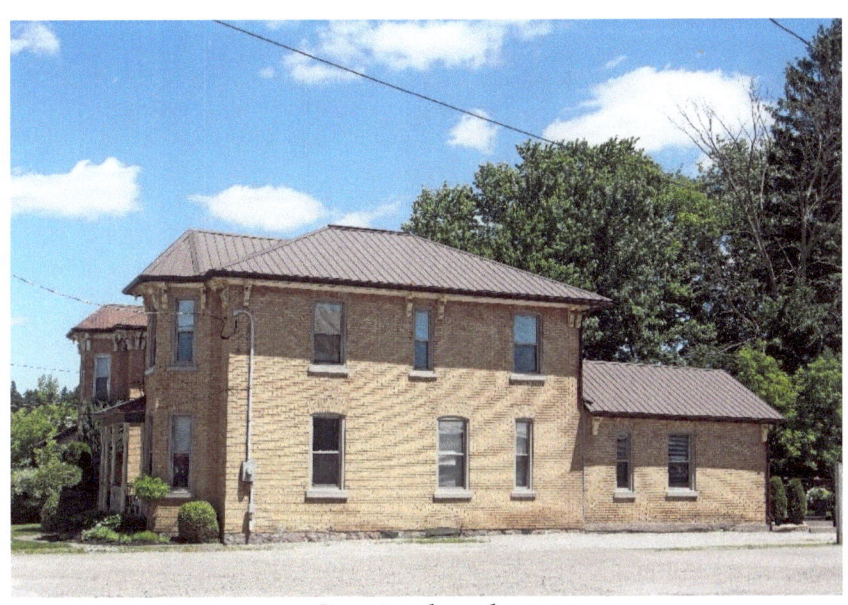

Cornice brackets

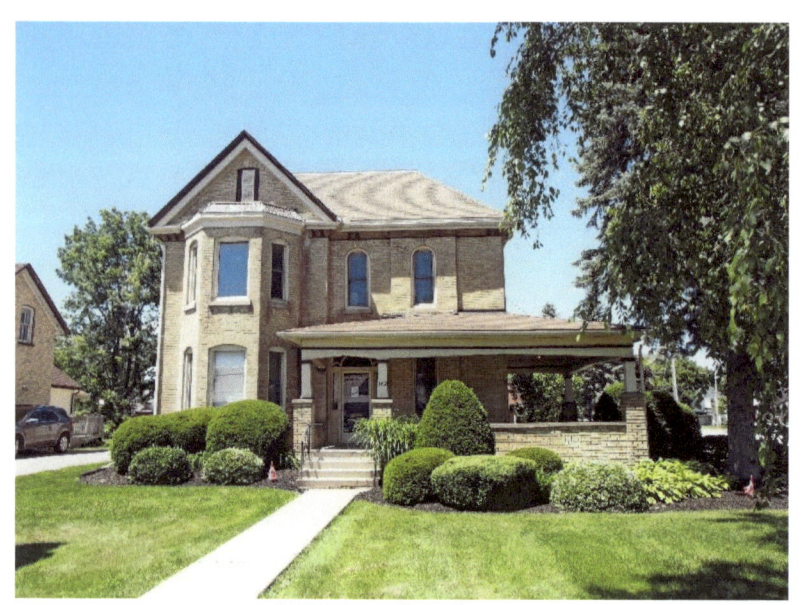
162 Dundas Street

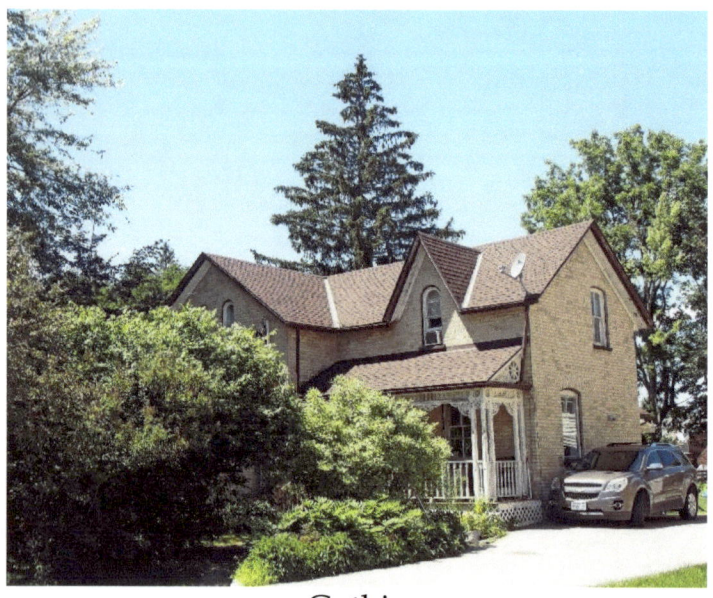
Gothic

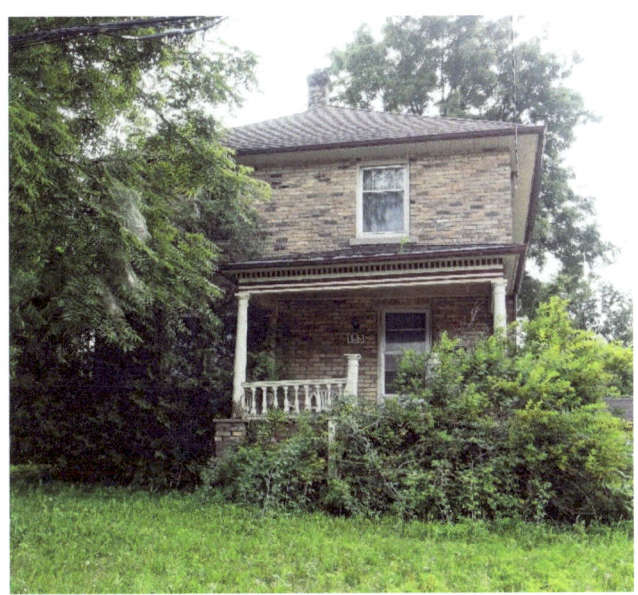

#153

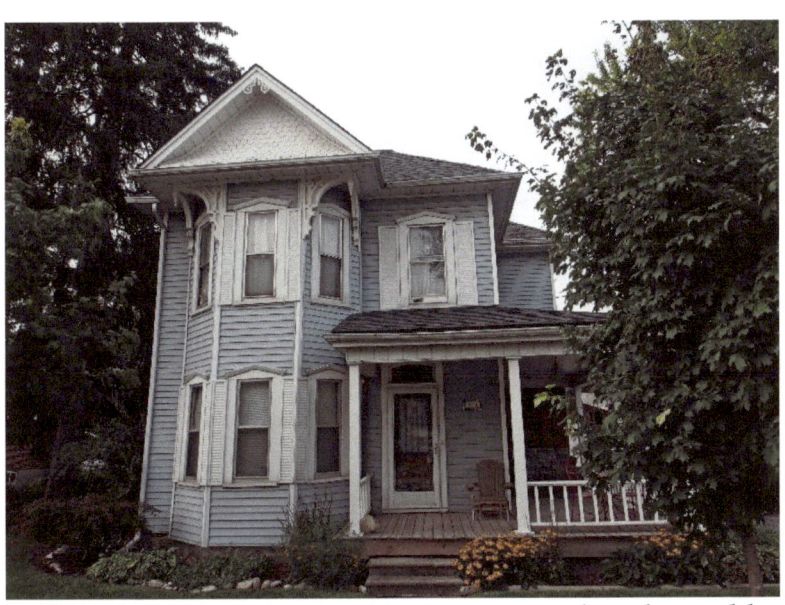

#174 – two-storey tower-like bay capped with a gable, fretwork

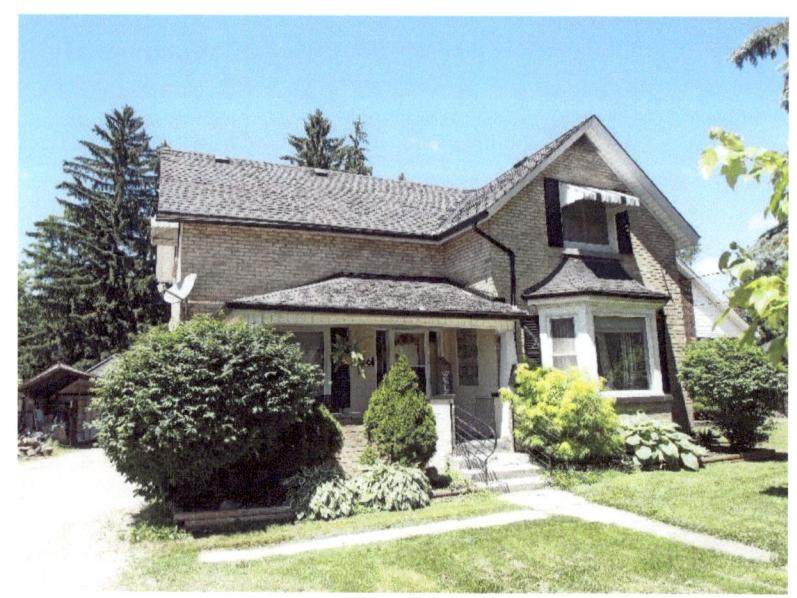

#186

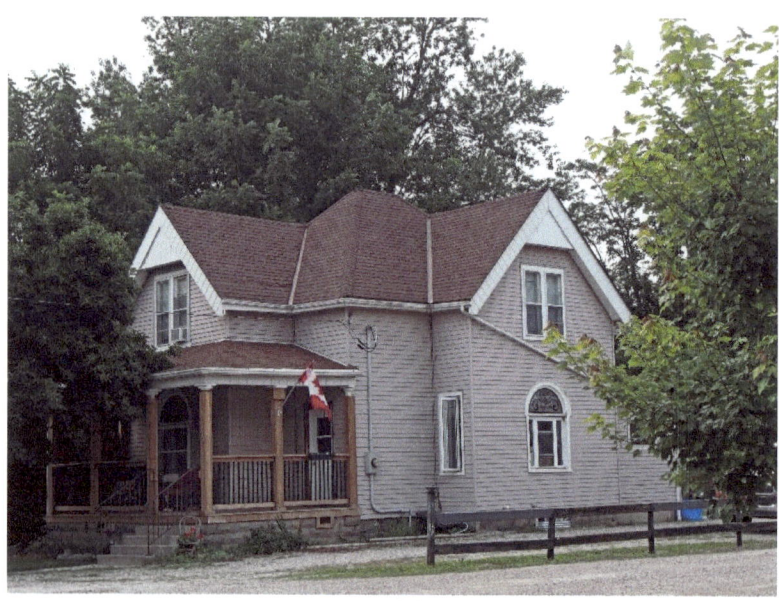

#190

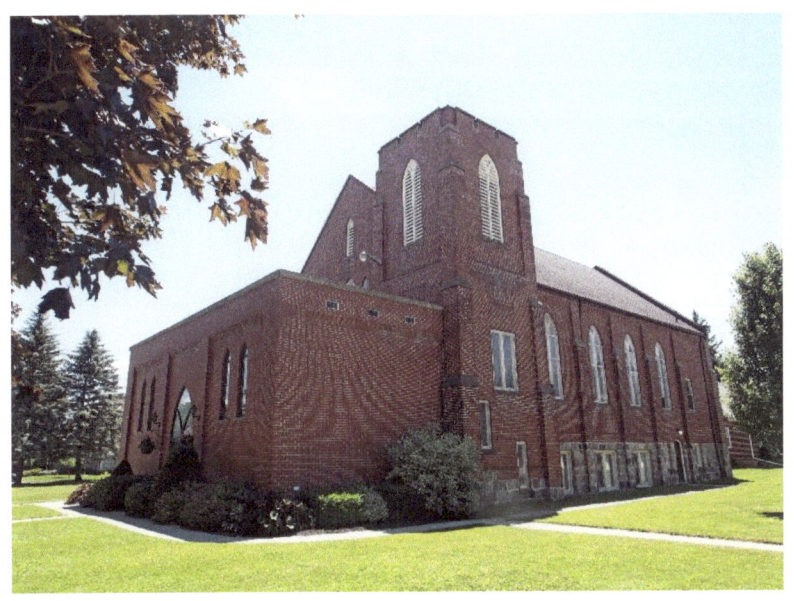

115 George Street – Westminster United Church

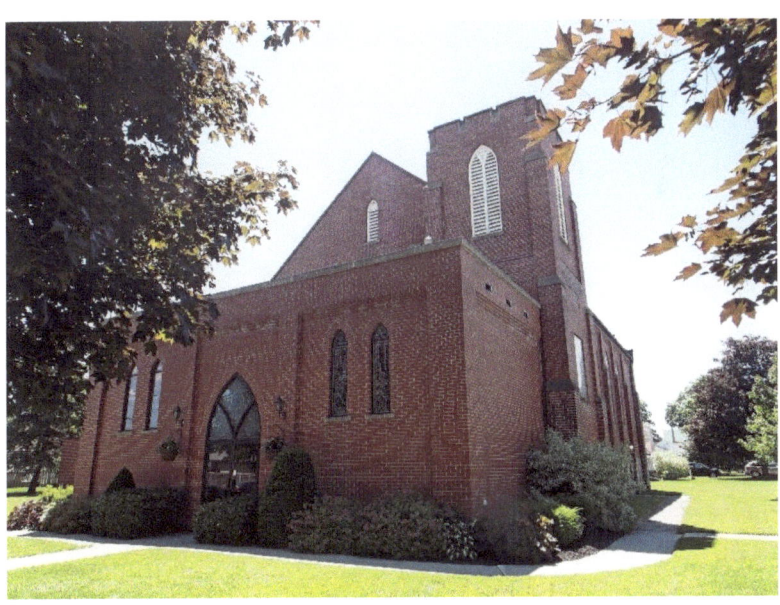

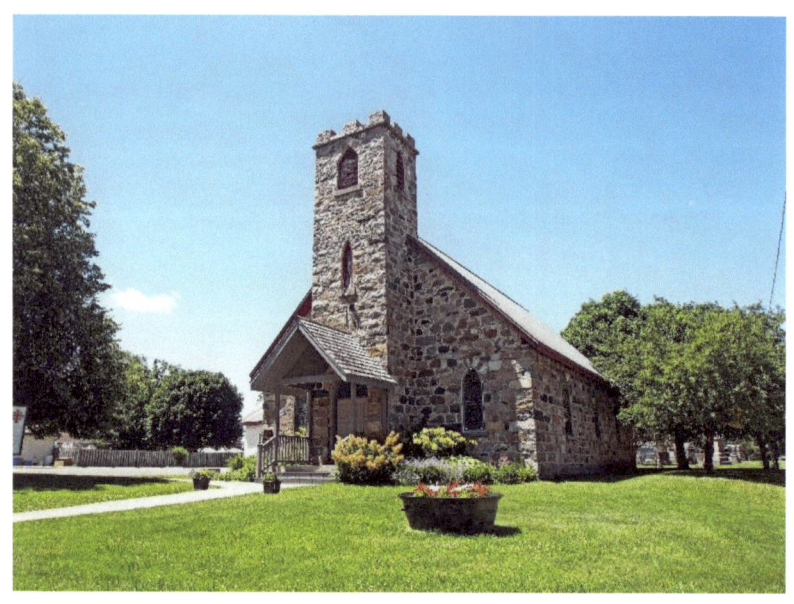

220 Dundas Street West – St. John's Anglican Church Thamesford – constructed with local field stones in 1862 – Gothic – lancet windows, battlementing on tower

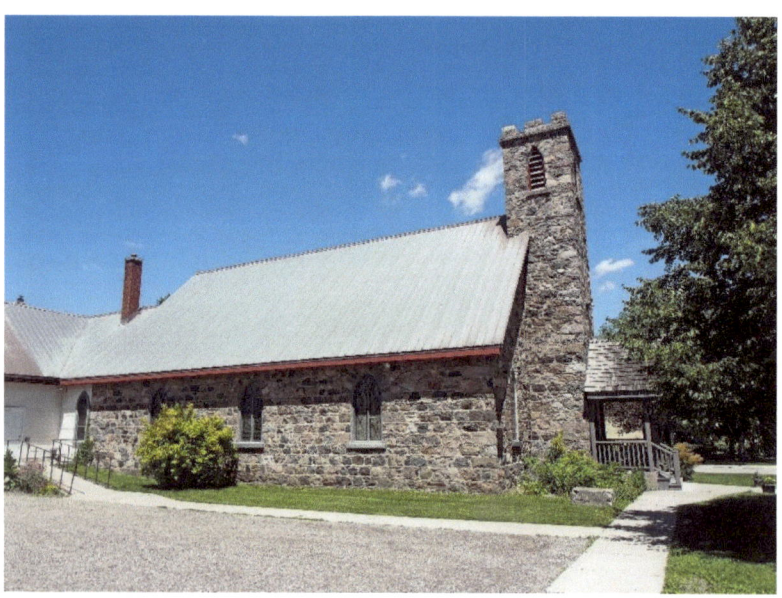

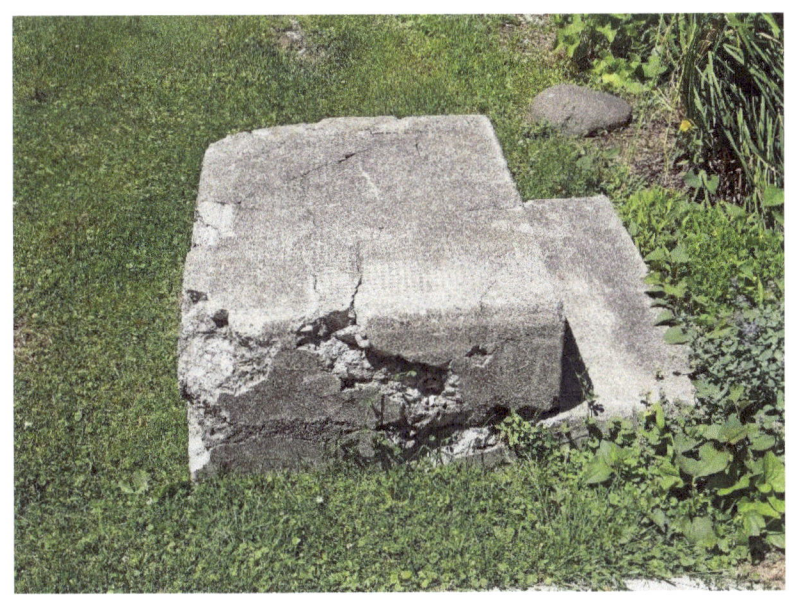

Original carriage alighting stone

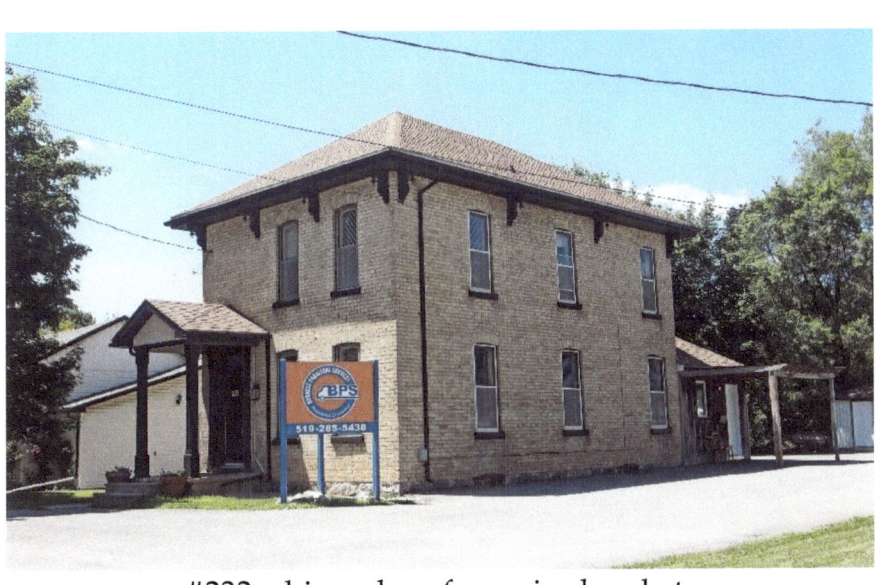

#232 – hipped roof, cornice brackets

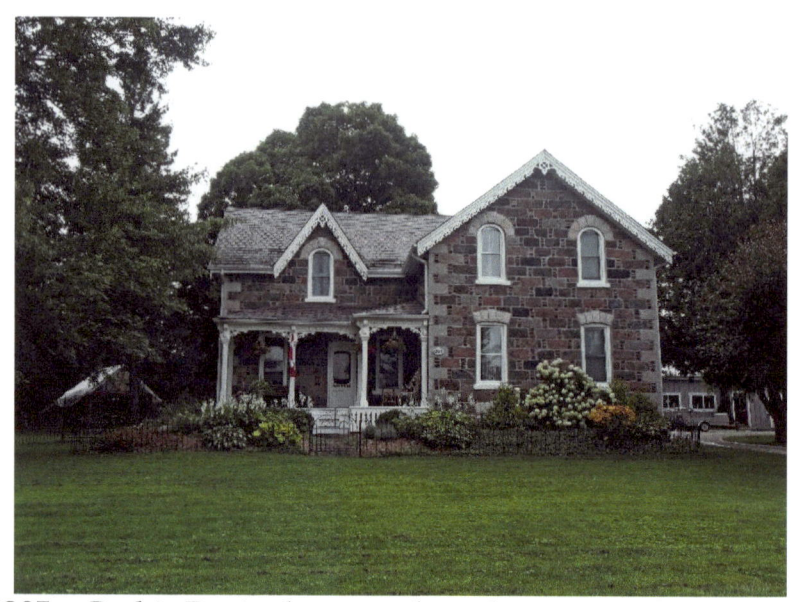

#205 – Gothic Revival – verge board trim on gables, corner quoins, voussoirs over windows

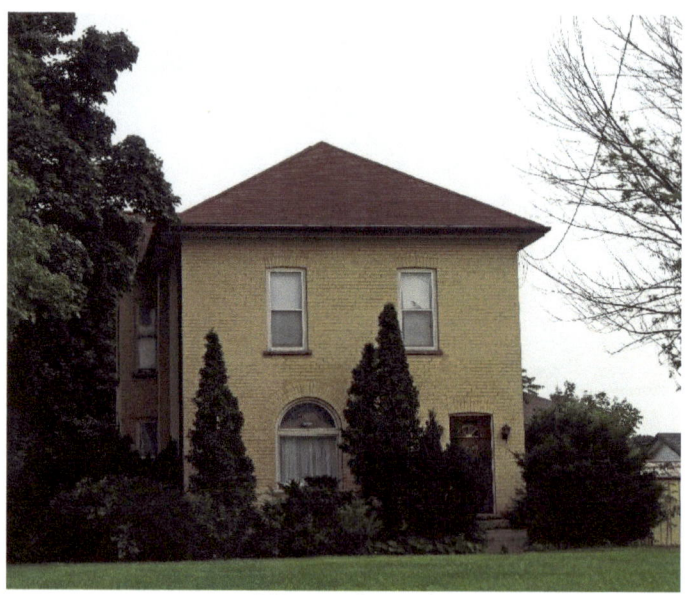

Hipped roof

Other Books by Barbara Raue

Coins of Gold
Arrows, Indians and Love
The Life and Times of Barbara
The Cromwell Family Book
Laura Secord Discovered
Daddy Where Are You?

Montana Series
Book 1: Montana Dream
Book 2: Life on the Montana Frontier
Book 3: Montana to Boston and Back
Book 4: Montana Sons Go to War
Book 5: Montana Sons Return from War

© 2019 by Barbara Raue - All the photos in this book have been taken with my cameras. I own the rights to them.

www.ingramcontent.com/pod-product-compliance
Lightning Source LLC
Chambersburg PA
CBHW040246220526
45473CB00001B/392